MISSISSIPPI:
the long, hot summer

MISSISSIPPI:
the long, hot summer

by William McCord

W · W · Norton & Company · Inc · *New York*

For Kirsten,
whose love, patience and
good humor made the long, hot summer bearable.

Acknowledgments:
Winter, 1964

As I write these last words, I am sitting by the Nile. The pyramids loom on the other bank. Here, on the shores of this river, man first developed the concept of human brotherhood. Mississippi is far away in spirit as well as fact, but the stories of its brutality conquer distance.

Several days ago, some Egyptian villagers asked me why white Americans treated Negroes so badly. I had no answer. Yesterday, a letter arrived from a Negro friend in Jackson saying that the shootings and cross-burnings had gotten worse. Today, news comes from McComb: a former student of mine, along with numerous town residents, has been jailed for possessing weapons. (Actually, the student is a pacifist.)

The trend of events makes one feel helpless. Like any "reasonable man," I know full well that the American government is most unlikely to act. The realists say, perhaps rightly, that the men who run America will not intervene in Mississippi until more and more killings force them to change their policy.

I hope, with this book, to have added to those voices of protest which may lead America to act before a final, violent debacle in the South. Unfortunately, I can thank publicly only a few of those people whose information and inspiration made this book possible: Aaron Henry, Bob and Donna Moses, Richard Jewett, Illene Steirlitz, Dennis Sweeney, James Silver; writers like Claude Sitton of *The New York Times* and the unknown editor of *Newsweek* whose superb articles enlightened the nation, and Christopher Knipp whose criticism sharpened, clarified, and enlivened the book.

And to those who must remain anonymous, I send my gratitude, my admiration, and my hope . . .

To Sally, Sandy, and GeeGee for all of their kindness,

To Rev. W. who had the courage to talk and to Mr. H. who had the courage to act,

To the McL's and all of the others who kept the watch,

To Landy who, I hope, will someday be just plain Landy again,

To the white people who have too long sat behind their closed curtains up on the Northside but who have finally sided with Negroes,

To Jackie, Dicky, Kim, and Eddy who will, I hope, live to see a better future.

WILLIAM MCCORD
Cairo, November, 1964

Table of Contents

A Personal Introduction

IN 1963, standing before the statue of "The Great Emancipator" in Washington, the Reverend Martin Luther King addressed thousands of Americans who had marched upon the capital to express their desire for liberty. "I have a dream," he said, "that one day even the state of Mississippi, a state sweltering in the heat of oppression, will be transformed into an oasis of freedom and justice."

During the long, hot summer of 1964—and the years which preceded it—thousands of Negro and white Americans fought to transform this dream into a reality. Some lost their property and jobs in this struggle, some suffered beatings and torture, many went to jail, and some died. Only future historians will be able to gauge the ultimate effect of these sacrifices, for anyone who has been to the "Black Belt" of the United States soon learns that this fortress of oppression may take generations to breach.

Yet even now, while many people throughout the world still recoil in disbelief from the outrages of 1964 (and a few gloat), one judgment may be ventured: the Mississippi Project has given indelible testimony to both the nobility and the brutality which reside in the heart of America. Knowing that their lives and the welfare of their children were at stake, thousands of Mississippi Negroes cast their lot with the cause of freedom. And from the North came hundreds of comrades, drawn mostly from that young generation raised in the soft era of the 1950's.

Many Southerners—most prominently, that brave Mississippi historian James Silver—also took their stand for freedom. But this idealism and wisdom too often found a counterpart in the sadism or, at best, sullen acquiescence of white Southerners.

This book records a simple narrative of one battle in the war to guarantee elementary rights to American Negroes. While I have attempted to portray certain of the reasons which prompted white Mississippians to maintain a system of oppression, no claim can be made for scholarly objectivity. Clearly, I believe in the justice of the Negro revolt and the right of Negroes to participate as full citizens in American society. The concerted and, until recently, successful maintenance of southern tyranny can be defended only by the most insensitive of bigots.

Writing this essay seemed worthwhile for several reasons. As a social scientist, I was naturally drawn to the job of depicting the Mississippi revolt as one illustration of America's most important social movement and of analyzing, as far as possible, the motives, actions, and beliefs of the protagonists. As an individual who has happened to witness (and criticize) totalitarian dictatorships in Europe, in Africa, and Asia, I wanted Americans to know the facts about our own form of dictatorship. Further, as a minor participant in the Mississippi events, I felt compelled to tell some of the stories of suffering and heroism which, for various reasons, have not always received proper attention in the national press.

The book has been written with a degree of passion and personal involvement. I hope the reader will forgive this scholarly lapse; the human meaning of the Mississippi revolt cannot be adequately conveyed in a textbook manner. It would do an injustice to those who have been killed and to those who carry on the battle to treat them as sociological data rather than as individual human beings.

While this social history is limited to Mississippi specifically and the South generally, Northerners must realize that the same sort of oppression victimizes the Negro throughout America. The discrimination—in schools, jobs, and housing—may be more subtle, less violent, and slightly more polite, but the effects are equally pernicious. Mississippi may seem a foreign land, but it *is* a part of America—and represents in a bitter capsule the prejudice which has ravaged our nation.

My own involvement in the "Negro question" came, as it does inevitably for all white Americans, quite early in life. I recall with guilt the Negro slums which encroached upon my childhood neighborhood in St. Louis, a border city which the southern mystique had impregnated. I remember, too, childish arguments with Negro children where, as an invincible rejoinder, I would yell: "What do you know? You're just a nigger!" Undoubtedly, I too played the role of the white oppressor whom Saunders Redding describes movingly in his essay, *On Being Negro in America*. Redding once watched his son as the boy first experienced the outrage of rejection from a white boy. The Negro boy asked:

> "Don't you want to play?"
> "I can't play with you," the white boy said.
> "What's the matter, are you sick?"
> "I just can't play with you any more."
> "Why?"
> "Because you're a nigger, that's why," the boy said.
> My son did not cry, but in his eyes was the look of a wound, and I knew it would grow, become infected, and pump its poison to every tissue, to every brain cell!

There can never be forgiveness or excuse for those of us who have made such attacks upon another's dignity.

With the coming of maturity, I tried to make meager amends through such insufficient means as picketing discriminatory employers, organizing civil rights projects, and conducting research into the myths about Negro intellectual inferiority and criminal propensities. Perhaps such efforts—and the thousands of civil and legal actions undertaken by other Americans during the last decade—may have done a little to reduce the American Negro's burden and to allay the white man's guilt. But these activities seemed quite inadequate as reports about white intransigence began to filter through the curtain of silence which has traditionally surrounded the southern tyranny. Little Rock, Birmingham, Montgomery, Albany—all suggested that a powerful urge to freedom had emerged in the South and that the white power elite would do all it could to stifle it.

The full extent of the southern oppression was most directly revealed to me in February of 1964, when a small group of Stanford faculty sat in the sheltered atmosphere of a Palo Alto home. We listened to Edward Vickery, a lanky Stanford student who told in subdued terms of mounted police charging and trampling southern Negro children. He talked of NAACP members in the Black Belt who disappeared at night without trace. He described the bombings which shook churches and, at times, took lives. Vickery had just returned from the deep South where he had helped Negroes in a voter registration drive. His activities had been peaceful and constitutional; essentially, he had encouraged Negro citizens to approach registrars with a request to vote. When they were refused, Vickery and his co-workers led picketing marches around the courthouse.

As we listened to his description of southern conditions, two ironic elements of the situation could not be ignored. First, Vickery, a brilliant, cultured student, wore the blue uniform of a prison inmate. One day his luck had run out, and he had been arrested on a variety of charges. One indictment included "trespassing on private property." The city council of a small town in

Louisiana had declared the village sidewalks to be private property; when Vickery walked down a street, police arrested him. In February he awaited trial after having secured temporary freedom on $18,000 bail. His Virginia family had disowned him and Vickery's fate remained highly uncertain.

A second fact about Vickery struck me with a more personal poignancy. While labeled as a northern "agitator," Vickery was the great-grandson of Stonewall Jackson. Almost to the month, one hundred years before, my own grandfather had been riding with Sherman. The Union troops had turned the Confederate flank in May of 1864 and had, so they thought, brought freedom to the slaves. Yet, here Vickery and I sat, the descendants of two enemies, discussing the ways freedom might finally be brought to the South. Vickery described the threats, shootings, and killings which plagued the Negro who sought his liberty in the South. He pleaded as a Southerner for aid from all the nation.

At Stanford, in April of 1964, the Reverend Martin Luther King and Robert Moses, a leader of Mississippi's civil rights movement, repeated the request for northern assistance. Mississippi was to serve as a focus: both as a symbol and in fact, the state was the citadel of southern authoritarianism. Robert Moses reported that there could be no hope for social justice in Mississippi "without the massive aid of the country as a whole, backed by the power and authority of the federal government." Years of struggle in the state indicated that opposition to change on the part of Mississippi's elite grew more stubborn as the years passed. "Negro efforts to win the right to vote," Moses said, "cannot succeed against the extensive legal weapons and police powers of local and state officials without a nationwide mobilization of support."

Bob Moses knew his subject well. Born in Harlem, this young leader abandoned his graduate work in philosophy at Harvard to come to Mississippi. He joined SNCC (the Student Nonviolent Coordinating Committee) as a voter registration worker in 1960. A specialist in mathematical logic, unassuming, slight of stature, and modest to the point of humility, Bob Moses did not fit the part of charismatic leader. Yet by 1964, he headed a massive state organization, COFO (the Council of Federated Organizations), which coordinated civil rights activities in Mississippi. When he and his colleagues issued a call for national aid, they spoke for a large majority of Mississippi's nearly one million Negroes.

Bob Moses reached his position of leadership not by flamboyance, but rather by being among the first to risk the punishment which Mississippi's power elite administers to "uppity" Negroes. For years he had suffered the consequences which befall the "agitator." On August 15, 1961, for example, a county official stopped Moses and three Negroes who had tried unsuccessfully to register to vote in Liberty. "Are you the man, who's been trying to register our niggers?" the officer asked. When Moses replied that he was, he was arrested, fined, and jailed for "impeding an officer in the discharge of his duties." Seven days later, Moses and his friends again tried to register. After being turned back, they walked a block from the Liberty courthouse. There, one Billy Jack Caston, the sheriff's first cousin, attacked Moses, a man pledged to nonviolence. It took eight stitches to bind up Moses's head. An all-white jury acquitted Billy Jack Caston of assault charges.

One year later, in Sunflower County, police arrested Moses and four other SNCC workers for passing out pamphlets door to door. The brochure announced a registration mass meeting in the county. The police charged Moses with "distributing literature without a permit"—by this time the Mississippi officials had effectively enforced anti-pamphleteering laws.

In September, 1962, in Ruleville, Moses and local Negroes established a voter registration office in a chapel. On September 3, as Moses and Amzie Moore, a town leader, walked down a street in Ruleville, a white man in a truck pulled up beside them. "Are you the folks getting the people to register?" When they replied affirmatively, the man said that he had a double-barreled shotgun waiting for them if they dared to come to his plantation to register

Negroes. The same day, Ruleville Mayor Durrough informed the Baptist Church that the chapel's tax exemption and free water had been cut off.

The intimidation continued in 1963 when Bob Moses and other registration workers were arrested in Greenwood. They had been picked out from a group of one hundred Negroes who had intended to register at the Greenwood courthouse. The police dispersed the voter aspirants with police dogs.

Later in 1963, Bob Moses investigated the bombing of the home of Hartman Turnbow, a Negro leader in Holmes County. Turnbow's house had been firebombed with Molotov cocktails. He and the white attackers shot at each other. Turnbow, Moses, and three other Negroes found themselves under arrest on the incredible charge that they had set fire to Turnbow's own home. The police could not find any white attackers.

In January of 1964, Moses suffered arrest again, this time in Hattiesburg where he tried to escort would-be voter registrants through a police cordon around the courthouse. The charge: breach of the peace. Local FBI agents said that they could take no action.

When Bob Moses talked at Stanford University in February of 1964, he did not mention these incidents or the other forms of constant harassment which endangered his life. Rather he outlined some modest plans for the coming summer. He and other COFO leaders hoped to accomplish four aims:

1. They wished to increase the number of Negroes registered to vote in the state. Only 25,000 Negroes had passed the barriers allowing them to vote, although Negroes comprised over 42 per cent of Mississippi's population.

2. COFO wanted to organize a "Freedom Democratic Party," made up of registered or disenfranchised citizens, which would challenge the power and patronage exercised by the regular Democratic party over the state.

3. They hoped that "Freedom Schools" would be established in

fifteen towns. These educational facilities were designed to teach
literacy, arithmetic, citizenship—even foreign languages—to
Negro youth.

4. Civil rights workers also envisaged the construction of community centers. The centers would provide job training, health
education, libraries, and meeting places for Negro citizens.

What reasonable man could argue with these objectives? In almost any civilized community, attempts to register voters and
extend educational and welfare services would have been welcomed. In the deep South, however, demagogues labeled the
program as "Communist," "subversive," and perhaps worst of all,
inspired by "outside agitators."

The "agitators" came to Mississippi. Out of thousands who applied—out of hundreds of thousands who expressed commendable
but unfulfilled longings to come—approximately one thousand
students, lawyers, ministers, and teachers arrived in the Magnolia
state during its "hospitality month" of June, 1964.

On both sides, people believed that the summer of 1964 could
prove the most crucial civil rights testing ground of the decade. If
Mississippi could be changed, the example might stir the entire
South. Civil rights leaders like John Lewis (chairman of SNCC—
the Student Nonviolent Coordinating Committee) said, "the summer of 1964 could really be *the* year for Mississippi. Before the
Negro people get the right to vote, there will have to be a massive
confrontation. . . . We are going to Mississippi in force."

Segregationist Allen Thompson, mayor of Jackson, felt equally
strongly. "This is it," he commented, "they are not bluffing and we
are not bluffing. We're going to be ready for them . . . they won't
have a chance."

Many of us felt that truly we would not have a chance—and for
some who fell in the battle this prophecy came true. And yet,
however filled with fear, thousands of Northerners and Southerners, Negro and white, felt compelled to participate in that long
hot summer. The reasons which lay behind this decision—the

spirit which informed the commitment—can be grasped only if one understands the nature of oppression, Mississippi style.

In my own case, two Negro children most explicitly exposed the effects of southern white dictatorship. One night, we sat on the lawn of a home in Jackson's Negro neighborhood. Languor and peace pervaded the evening, a slight breeze ruffled the trees, and dogs wrestled playfully in the grass. We talked of the many things which interest children—of cowboys and soldiers, of animals and the delights of watermelon. Dickie, a four-year-old boy with fair skin and dimpled cheeks, asked:

"How much is a dollar? What all can you buy with it?

"Twenty ice-cream cones," I said.

"That's right," his five-year-old sister put in, "but now you be sure, boy, not to get them from a white man in a white truck."

"Why not?"

"Because that man in the white truck, he could throw a bomb on you. You got to go buy your ice cream only from a brown man in a brown truck. He don't throw no bombs."

With that, she snuggled closer, somehow ignoring my white skin. This, at base, is why the "invasion of Mississippi" took place: to release children from the fear that ice-cream trucks carry bombs.

MISSISSIPPI:
the long, hot summer

1

Prelude to "Invasion": 1954 to 1964

By February of 1964, all the major civil rights organizations had joined together to attack Mississippi's bastions of segregation. The Congress of Racial Equality (CORE), the Student Nonviolent Coordinating Committee (SNCC), the Southern Christian Leadership Conference (SCLC), the NAACP, and even the National Council of Churches announced their intention of mounting a coordinated attack. This cooperation in itself evidenced a new spirit, for the variety of people and philosophies embodied in these organizations had never before been brought together in common cause.

In a joint public statement issued by COFO (the umbrella federation which loosely covered the various groups), Robert Moses, James Farmer, and James Forman said, "after three years of struggling, accompanied by extreme harassment in Mississippi, COFO has decided that only by confrontation within the state of the civil rights movement and the forces maintaining the *status quo* can significant change in the social and legal structure be effected." The leaders called for a large number of volunteers "who are willing to commit their beings as well as their minds to our common struggle." They concluded that "mere sympathy from a distance has proven insufficient to match the intransigence of the state of Mississippi." [1]

Some voices from the white community joined the Negro leadership in urging national assistance and attention. On April 15, 1964, twelve University of Mississippi professors, at no little risk to their jobs, wrote to their colleagues across the nation: "It is of vital importance that the facts be made known, because the state is such a crucial testing ground in the struggle to expand and improve American democracy." The majority of Mississippi Negroes and many of the state's wiser whites had come to the reluctant conclusion that their society, like Nazi Germany, had lost the will for moral regeneration. As historian James Silver, of the University, wrote in his eloquent book, *Mississippi: The Closed Society,* "As yet there is little evidence that the society of the closed mind will ever possess the moral resources to reform itself, or the capacity for self-examination, or even the tolerance of self-examination." [2]

This rather desperate conclusion had been forced upon the enlightened part of the Mississippi community. Beginning in 1954 with the school desegregation decision, an uneven and often unreported battle had been waged against the Mississippi *status quo*. Tragically, after a decade, men of good will came to the point where they believed that only a demonstration of the national presence might bring about significant progress. Parts of the sorrowful story of this decade must be recounted here in order to comprehend why the Mississippi revolt of 1964 took place.

Democracy in Mississippi: "Terror Hangs over the Negro"

In 1876, Senator Blanche Bruce, one of the two Negro senators from Mississippi during the Reconstruction period, eloquently condemned the practices of his state. After an election marked by open violence and the re-establishment of white supremacy, Bruce observed, "the conduct of the late election in Mississippi . . . put in question and jeopardy the sacred rights of the citizens . . . the evidence on hand . . . will show beyond peradventure that in many parts of the State corrupt and violent influences were brought to bear upon the registrars of voters . . . and upon the masses of voters in such measures and strength as to produce grave apprehensions for personal safety and as to deter them from the exercise of their political franchises." [3]

Bruce's words have a modern flavor, for little has changed with the passage of time. In 1963, the Mississippi Advisory Committee to the U.S. Commission on Civil Rights reported that "in all important areas of citizenship, a Negro in Mississippi receives substantially less than his due consideration as an American and as a Mississipian. We find that terror hangs over the Negro in Mississippi and is an expectancy for those who refuse to accept their color as a badge of inferiority." [4]

Throughout the last decade, the Negro in Mississippi has been systematically deprived of his right to vote by rigged laws, chicanery, economic harassment, physical violence, and death. Any objective person who reviews the evidence from 1954 to 1964 cannot avoid this verdict. Let me record just a few out of the hundreds of acts of intimidation which kept the black man "in his place."

In 1955 the Reverend G. W. Lee, a Negro citizen of Belzoni, had been active in registering Negroes to vote. On the night of May 7, unidentified men shot and killed Lee as he drove along a country road. Another Negro activist in Belzoni, Gus Courts, was shot and seriously wounded on November 26, 1955. Courts, an ex-president of the state NAACP, finally fled the state. Another Negro from the same region, Lemar Smith, was shot to death at noon, August 13, in front of a courthouse.

The use of violence as a weapon of white policy temporarily served its purpose. In 1956, not a single new Negro voter was added to the polling lists. Only 4 per cent of eligible Negroes had received the franchise as opposed to 41 per cent of the whites. By some—perhaps pessimistic—estimates the number of Negro voters dropped to an all-time low of 8,000 people in 1956.[5]

Nevertheless, in 1956, Negroes may have felt a breath of hope when the U.S. Justice Department began its first investigations of complaints that Negroes had been unfairly disqualified from voting. Their findings could hardly be in doubt in a state where the Governor, J. P. Coleman, publicly announced that Negroes were not fit to vote and the chairman of the Democratic Executive Committee, J. J. Tubb, stated in 1955 that "We don't intend to have any Negroes voting in this primary." [6] The whites imposed their will so effectively that even Negro college teachers and Fellows of the National Science Foundation failed to qualify for the vote.

By 1961 the Justice Department had gathered sufficient evidence to lodge suits against Mississippi's voter registrars. On July 6, the Justice Department sued to ban discrimination against Negroes in Clarke and Forrest Counties. In Clarke, not one of the county's 3,000 Negroes had been permitted to register while a substantial majority of whites had been given the vote. In Forrest, only 25 out of 7,500 eligible Negroes had been enfranchised. Other suits followed.

Perhaps encouraged by the possibility of Federal supervision of elections, an increasing number of Negroes in the early 1960's tried to assert their constitutional right. For the first time in Mississippi, Negroes launched open protests, lawsuits and peaceful marches as means of changing their politically powerless station in life. In every area of the state, they met with unrelenting hostility.[7] A few examples give some indication of this reign of terror.

On September 7, 1961, at Tylertown, John Hardy, a SNCC worker, escorted two Negroes to the courthouse. As Hardy describes the scene, the registrar informed them that he "wasn't registering voters that day." As the three walked toward the door, the registrar, John Q. Wood, pulled a pistol and hit Hardy on the head from behind. Police arrested the Negro for "disturbing the peace." On September 25, at Liberty, white state representative E. H. Hurst killed Herbert Lee, a Negro who had taken leadership in voter registration. The authorities did not prosecute Hurst.

White persecution of Negroes continued in 1962. During the summer, for example, a registration drive gained momentum in Leflore County. The whites responded by cutting off the distribution of federally supplied food and by arresting and shooting voter registration workers. County officers used police dogs to curb Negro marches, and judges sentenced eight people to serve prison terms. Fire destroyed the county's registration drive headquarters and its records of Negro aspirants for the vote. The mayor and commissioners of Greenwood officially charged that the Negroes had set fire to their own headquarters and that the registration workers had been shooting each other.

In every part of the state, between 1961 and 1963, the white community applied illegal and pseudo-legal methods of coercion:

In Rankin County, the local sheriff admitted in Federal court that he had beaten D. M. Grim, a Negro registration worker. The sheriff exhibited pride in his prowess: "I hit him as many times as I could. If he hadn't run, I'd have kept on hitting him." [8]

In Madison County, shotgun fire injured five Negroes as they walked away from a voter registration meeting. As in the vast majority of the instances of violence, the police could not find any clue as to the identity of the assailants.

And even in Jackson, the capital of Mississippi and the state's most industrialized, progressive city, force had to be used to control the Negro population. On May 31, 1963, Jackson police clubbed Willie Lunden, NAACP official, as he led a group of Negroes from a church. Police arrested 421 demonstrators and imprisoned them at the Hinds County fairgrounds.[9]

The beatings, arrests and harassments temporarily served their purpose in denying most Negroes formal access to Mississippi poli-

tics. In 1963, however, civil rights leaders created a novel "underground election" as a way of giving Negroes a channel of expression in the gubernatorial elections. They nominated Aaron Henry,
a Negro, as governor and the Reverend Edwin King, a white minister, to lead an underground ticket. In the "freedom vote," everyone over twenty-one could cast a ballot. Aaron Henry received
82,000 votes, a highly significant tally when one considers the
techniques used by whites to frustrate the "mock election." Nearly
every worker in the campaign suffered arrest or detainment.[10]

Aaron Henry, the man who led the freedom election, withstood
all the pressures which befalls a Negro who tries to change the
southern way of life. A former shoeshine boy, Henry eventually
established his own drugstore in Clarksdale. Thugs smashed his
store windows innumerable times, but amidst the debris he still
displayed the Declaration of Independence and the Emancipation
Proclamation. On March 13, 1963, gasoline bombs set Henry's
home ablaze. Two young whites admitted the bombing but said they
"were just having fun." An all-white jury acquitted the arsonists.
One of them later asked Henry to forgive him. In May, 1963, an
explosion ripped Henry's drugstore. Fire inspectors declared that
lightning caused the explosion.[11]

While the Henry election had no bearing on official returns, it
did indicate that Negroes had the will and capacity to engage in the
electoral process. The Freedom vote dramatized the authoritarianism of Mississippi's political affairs and gave an unprecedented
voice to Negro demands for social justice, equal opportunity and
free elections.

By 1964, the whites ran scared as the demand for free elections
spread even more widely in the Negro community. On January 23,
Canton police searched a community registration center and seized
a list of names from a petition. Officers arrested two persons for
making repairs on the building and, later in the day, arrested nine
more workers for "distributing leaflets without a permit." The
brochures urged Negroes to pay the poll tax. The court set bail at
$800 each. On January 31, in Liberty, someone shot and killed

Negro Louis Allen. Allen had been a witness to the earlier killing of Herbert Lee by a Mississippi legislator. During the summer, a Liberty policeman had beaten Allen with a flashlight, breaking his jaw.

On Freedom day in Hattiesburg, police arrested Oscar Chase, a SNCC worker, on a traffic violation. Jailers watched as white prisoners beat "the nigger-lover." As Chase remembered the incident: "I could see the jailer and some other policemen looking at me and grinning. I could also see the other prisoner standing over me, kicking me. I began to get up, was knocked down again, and then heard the door of the cell open . . ." Later, he remembered: "I saw the trusty put a pack of cigarettes and some matches under the door of my attacker's cell. . . . I heard the police come in and let him out. I could hear them laughing." [12]

These case studies in intimidation, torture, and death could fill an entire book, but the case against Mississippi seems clear: In the face of a simple request to vote, Negroes and whites have been clubbed, shot and killed. Using every weapon at their disposal, the whites have mercilessly maintained their political supremacy. Norman Thomas summed up the indictment against Mississippi. Thomas, who spoke in Greenwood during the Freedom campaign, wrote to the late President Kennedy:

We have in Mississippi a state obsessed with maintenance of segregation in support of white supremacy. It is a religion which, like communism to its believers, cleanses and sanctifies lies, perjury, perversion of law, perhaps even murder to maintain itself. This situation is America's business. I do not write as a sensationalist, but as a veteran campaigner who has frequently covered the United States without finding a parallel or precedent for what I found in Mississippi.[13]

Justice in Mississippi: "A Pernicious Difference"

"There are four laws in Mississippi," a common saying in the state goes. "One for whites against whites, another for Negroes versus Negroes, a third for the white who attacks a Negro, and the last for a Negro who has a grievance against a white." Except for the most hypocritical publicists, nobody has maintained that a Negro can expect equal treatment under the law in Mississippi. Thus, a second goal of the revolt in the state has been to establish a legal system which would assure some equity to the Negro.

Throughout the state, in COFO and NAACP offices, hang posters picturing a steel-helmeted, stern-faced member of the highway patrol. Underneath the portrait, a question has been posed: "Does he protect you?" The query is rhetorical since everyone in the state knows how the white man's justice has been applied. A few of the lesser-known incidents of recent years illustrate how Mississippi has interpreted the American ideal of "equal treatment under the law." In case after case, the usual protection assumed in other states—the right to immediate arraignment, the right to know the charge, the right to counsel, the right to expect immunity from police brutality—has been cynically, systematically, and consciously withheld.

Some examples:

On December 26, 1961, Rafford Johnson, a Negro, had a minor collision with a car driven by a white woman. Jackson police arrested Johnson and beat him severely. He later underwent brain surgery for injuries to his head.

On June 21, 1962, Clarksdale police arrested four students and a lawyer, William Higgs, who had been involved in integrationist activities. Imprisoned on a Sunday night, the four remained in jail for twenty hours. They were denied outside communication and were finally released without any charges having been filed against them.

On July 5, 1962, two SNCC workers, Jesse Harris, twenty, and Luvaghn Brown, seventeen, observed a trial in the Jackson courthouse.

According to affidavits by Harris and Brown, what occurred was as follows:

Officials told them to move from a bench traditionally used by whites. When the young Negroes refused, the court sentenced them to thirty days in jail. The two men later testified that they had been beaten and threatened with death because of their "crime." In the courthouse elevator, a deputy sheriff beat Harris on the head while calling him "a damned nigger." At the county farm, guards dressed them in conspicuous uniforms to indicate that they had been freedom riders. Guards beat both prisoners. One officer Keith shouted, "Nigger, I'll kill you," as he whipped Harris with a hose while other prisoners held him.

During August of 1962, Greenwood police arrested a fourteen-year-old boy, Welton McSwine, charging him with burglary of a white woman's house. His white employer eventually secured the boy's release. Before he left the jail, however, McSwine said that police beat him on the head with a blackjack, repeatedly hit him in the stomach with a club, and whipped him while he lay naked on a cell floor.

In March, 1963, again in Greenwood, hoodlums shot into the home of Dewey Greene, Sr., father of a boy who had recently applied to the University of Mississippi. Two other Greene children had participated in voter registration activities. The police said they would investigate the shotgun blast, but so far they have been unable to produce any suspects.

On June 18, 1963, forty-five Negroes walked to the home of Itta Bena's town marshal to request protection after their church had been gasbombed. Instead of offering protection, the police arrested the Negroes for "disturbing the peace." A justice of the peace fined them and sentenced them to six months in jail.

The agents of Mississippi justice reserve perhaps their most severe vindictiveness for white "nigger-lovers." Richard Jewett, a tall, red-haired electrical engineer, has received again and again the treatment which civil rights workers have learned to expect in Mississippi. After graduation from M.I.T., Jewett went to work for

CORE in Mississippi. On March 30, 1964, Jewett walked down a Jackson street, appropriately entitled Lynch Street, with a Negro girl, Miss Helen O'Neal. Jewett's experience with Jackson police can best be stated in the words of his own affidavit:

> We left the drugstore and started to walk back to the COFO office. . . . Just after walking by the Masonic Temple at 1072 Lynch Street we passed by a police prisoner van. . . .
>
> After we had walked perhaps twenty steps beyond the police car we heard a call of "Hey" behind us . . . the officer asked what I had been drinking. I replied, "Nothing." The officer said something like "nonsense" and then, "Come along with me."
>
> The van was then driven to the Jackson Police Station, the police car following close behind. . . . After the form had been completed, the officer started asking other questions. . . .
>
> We had moved to a desk on another side of the room where my pockets had been emptied and several questions had been asked about the contents of my pockets. . . . After this business with the pockets we had moved back to the desk with the typewriters, and the officers were arranged with two behind me and two in front of me.
>
> The officer who began to hit me was standing behind me. He raised his arm and came down with the side of his hand across my neck. . . . As he hit me the first time he said something like "Nigger-lover," but said nothing for each of the other blows.
>
> After these blows, the officer turned me slightly towards him and started to hit me in the body and stomach and face with his fists. As he did this he forced me back the six or eight feet across the room until I was against the wall. He then took my head in one of his hands and slammed it against the wall two or three times. After this he pulled me forward and forced me to the ground. While I was on the ground he kicked me several times in the stomach and chest.
>
> I then got up, and he started hitting me on the body again with his fists. He also kicked up with his leg several times and kicked me in the stomach. . . .[14]

Police charged Jewett with drunkenness and vagrancy. Jewett, a man known not to drink, testified that officer Earl Guess had led the beating. Officer Guess has yet to answer for the beating.

The ordeals which Jewett and other victims have undergone

occur almost daily. Most lawyers in the state, as well as ordinary citizens, either accept these events as routine procedure or somehow blind themselves to facts which even a casual visitor soon discovers. A few cases—the killing of Emmet Till, the lynching of Mack Parker, the assassination of Medgar Evers, and the murder of the three freedom fighters near Philadelphia, Mississippi, received national attention. Such events could not be blithely ignored. While these atrocities may have shocked the world, they received the applause of many Southerners. These were murders and widely reported. There is no need to review them in detail here. Suffice it to say that though there were eyewitnesses, incontrovertible evidence, and even post-trial confessions, no one to date has been convicted of these crimes. The Philadelphia case is pending at the time of this writing.

Whatever the offense—from traffic violation to murder—a white Mississippian can anticipate the most fraternal handling from his fellow Caucasians, particularly if he is charged with a crime against a "nigger." The Negro, on the other hand, has come to expect that his constitutional rights will more often than not be denied by the courts or flaunted by police and vigilantes. The Negro lives in a world of white brutality, white supremacy, and white law; it is a world where the policeman, the attorney, and the judge become symbols of terror. The Mississippi Advisory Committee to the U.S. Commission on Civil Rights has, in a somewhat understated form, summarized the administration of justice in Mississippi:

> From the moment a Negro adult is hailed as "boy" or "girl" by a police officer, through his arrest, detention, trial . . . and eventual imprisonment, he is treated with a pernicious difference. This difference is incompatible with Christian ideals about the dignity of man and with principles of Anglo-Saxon law.[15]

It is an interesting footnote to local feelings of guilt and self-protection that when Medgar Evers was gunned down in front of his home, the Jackson newspapers hinted that civil rights groups or some "outside agitator" had killed Evers. When Byron de la Beckwith, born in California, but resident in Mississippi for thirty-eight years, was arrested, the *Jackson Clarion-Ledger* felt compelled to produce the headline: "CALIFORNIAN IS CHARGED WITH MURDER OF EVERS."

By 1964, COFO workers hoped to make some progress toward the establishment of a rule of law in Mississippi. The reasons for their concern have been well stated by the Reverend Emil G. Hattoon. "You asked what the point of it is," he wrote to his two sons who had inquired why he fought for Negro rights, "I think the point is that this is much like Germany at the beginning of Hitler's rise—fear, police intimidation and summary arrests. I don't want you, or any other kids, to grow up in America in those circumstances."

Education in Mississippi:
Separate and Unequal

By the summer of 1964, Mississippi remained the only state in the Union which had not brought about even token integration in its primary and secondary school system. A decade earlier, Mississippi had announced its determined opposition to the Supreme Court's decision that segregated schooling was inherently illegal, as politicians invoked the sacred states' rights doctrine. In 1954, the first Citizens' Councils banded together to fight "the Communist theory of one world, one race"; this "uptown Klan" immediately achieved a membership of 80,000 persons. In 1955, the legislature passed a bill providing fines and jail sentences even for white children who attended Negro schools. In 1956, the legislature voted unanimously to declare the desegregation decision "invalid." Succeeding governors have sworn to uphold segregation and promised, if necessary, to close the public schools rather than integrate them.

At times, this oratory was tempered with the claim that the state had provided fine schools for Negroes—indeed even more modern facilities than those offered to white children. There has in fact been a flurry of Negro school building since 1954 in an effort to give some meaning to this boast. Nonetheless, the substance of the claim can best be evaluated in a 1962 report released by State Superintendent for Education J. M. Tubb.[16] The compilation showed wide disparities in the expenditure of school districts for white versus Negro pupils. On the state level, the study indicated that white children got an average of $81.86 while Negroes received $21.77.*

In a few urban areas, expenditures were close to equal; thus the city of Jackson spent $149.64 for white children and $106.37 for Negroes. Astounding inequities appeared most prominently in rural regions where Negroes comprised a high proportion of the population:

School Expenditures per Pupil in Rural Mississippi Districts

District	White	Negro	Negroes in the Population
Amite county	70.46	2.24	54.2%
Bolivar county No. 1	125.10	2.32	67.8%
Carrol county	81.26	7.08	58.2%
Holly Bluff	191.17	1.26	unknown
Jefferson county	96.29	2.60	75.5%
Tunica county	172.80	5.99	79.2%
Yazoo county	245.55	2.92	59.4%

In the face of such inequality, Negroes have naturally achieved a lower level of educational attainment. In 1960, for example, all Negroes over twenty-five had completed an average of only six years of school, five years less than the whites. While 168,000 whites had graduated from high school, only 16,000 Negroes had been awarded a secondary diploma.[17]

* The figures refer to local district expenditures. The state matches these sums on a dollar-for-dollar basis.

The white power elite has dedicated itself to the maintenance of this system. Politicians today faithfully reflect the attitudes of ex-Governor James K. Vardaman, who thoroughly understood that education of Negroes threatened the white position. Vardaman knew that the educated Negro would become dissatisfied with his destined position in society and would seek equality of opportunity. "Education would be a positive unkindness to him," Vardaman declared. "It simply renders him unfit for the work he will be forced to perform." Vardaman regarded the Negro as "a lazy, lying, lustful animal, which no amount of training can transform into a tolerable citizen." [18]

In his defense of school segregation nearly fifty years later, Governor Ross Barnett echoed Vardaman in a last stand against school integration. According to Barnett's never-never land logic, "If we start off with the self-evident proposition that the whites and colored are different, we will not experience any difficulty in reaching the conclusion that they are not and never can be equal." [19] The white opposition to the Supreme Court decision has been somewhat more bluntly stated by Medford Evans, a Citizens' Council leader: "Race-mixing is as irreversible a process as scrambling an egg. Easy to do, impossible to undo." Reasoning that school integration would lead to total "race mixture," Evans advised his followers in 1964: "If that is what the law requires, then the law be damned!" [20]

To ensure the stability of the *status quo,* whites have used every weapon available in their arsenal: interminable legal delays, economic intimidation of Negroes who have attempted to follow the Supreme Court order, and when all else failed, violence. On the other side, men of integrity and children of courage have been produced again and again by the Negro community in its battle to achieve educational opportunity. The experience of two Mississippi towns, Carthage and Yazoo, illustrates how this uneven combat has been waged.

Carthage lies in the red-earth hill country north of Jackson. The area has long been a center for white "crackers" and the KKK. Yet Carthage has also been known as a gathering spot for independent Negro farmers. Scattered around Carthage, particularly in the "Harmony Community," are neat fields and well-painted houses cared for by a Negro yeomanry. Blessed with relative self-sufficiency, this community has often exhibited the New England virtues of courage, parsimony, and a desire for education. Before the Supreme Court decision, the Negro farmers built with their own hands a cluster of buildings to serve as a school center. The school contained a library and an auditorium building as well as regular classrooms. After the integration order of 1954, the whites in Carthage apparently decided that the existence of an independent, Negro-governed school might become a source of subversion in the county. Without recompense, the whites dismissed the Negro board of trustees and absorbed the Harmony school into the regular system. Simultaneously, the town organized a White Citizens' Council, revamped its KKK, and began a strict surveillance of Harmony Negroes.

In an area where many of the farmers' homes display pictures of their children graduating from college, the new hope inspired by the Supreme Court decision could not easily be kept down. After a series of community meetings, the Negroes decided to present some test cases before the courts. The several families who pursued these suits immediately found themselves in economic difficulty. In some cases, upon hearing that a family had pushed for integration, county officers cut off aid to dependent children and federal supplies of surplus food. And the more prosperous Negro farmers suddenly found themselves blocked from their normal sources of seeds and supplies, while distributors refused to receive their goods for sale. Such economic harassment forced some families to leave the area and others to drop their integration suits. A few, however, continued to press for desegregated facilities.

By the 1960's economic intimidation gave way to open violence. KKK bands swarmed the back roads, burning crosses at the homes

of Negroes who advocated integration. Cars passing in the night
fired into Negro homes. The Negroes responded by setting up a
self-defense system. Each home had shotguns in readiness and was
joined to other farms in a well-planned defense "block." If unidentified cars entered an area, messengers sounded an alert and
armed farmers convened near the place where an attack might be
expected. Natural obstacles supplemented this defense. Many of
the more isolated farms, for example, put up electrified barbed
wire. It served the double purpose of keeping cows from straying
and preventing the invasion of night intruders.

This sturdy defiance of white intimidators gave strength to the
community. In 1964, a Negro candidate for Congress dared to run
for office from the area, and the Harmony group gave every indication that it would not give up the battle for school integration. One
widow, almost destitute from white economic harassment, still had
a suit pending in federal court. Although her son, aided by neighbors, had to stand guard every night and crosses had been burned
in front of her house, she continued to ask the court for her rights.
"They will never get us to turn back," she said, when I stayed with
the family in 1964. And her son, fondling his shotgun, added,
"The next time they burn a cross here, I'll know who done it—
because I'll find them out there in the morning." School desegregation had not come to Carthage as yet, but few in the community
doubted that the time would soon arrive when Negro children,
perhaps accompanied by federal marshals, could walk into white
Carthage schools.

The unified spirit so desperately maintained in Carthage has
been hard to find in most parts of Mississippi. The events in Yazoo
City serve as a more common example of the Negroes' tribula-
tions. Yazoo City, like the state, has a population equally divided
between whites and Negroes (in 1900, Yazoo Negroes outnumbered whites three to one, but a steady emigration has nar-
rowed the ratio). In 1955, the NAACP chose Yazoo City as one
of five towns to serve as target spots for school desegregation. In

one sense, this was a wise choice, for the city's record clearly indicated the fallacy of a "separate but equal" doctrine. The county spent 81 times as much money on the education of whites as on that of Negroes, while Yazoo City itself expended its school funds on a three-to-one basis favoring white children.

In another sense, however, Yazoo may have been a bad choice. The city stands at the gateway of the cotton-growing Delta region, where the plantation system has barely changed since the Civil War. Its Negroes have little of the economic independence of Carthage farmers and must depend largely upon white favor for their incomes. Despite this lack of an economic base the local NAACP chapter circulated a petition among Negroes, requesting school integration. Fifty-three families signed and submitted it to the local school board. The petition jolted Yazoo City whites out of a complacent assumption that Negroes would support a segregated system, and it sparked an increase in White Citizens' Council membership from 16 in 1954 to 1,430 by 1955.

The town reacted quickly and efficiently. The Yazoo City *Herald* published the names of all fifty-three petitioners. The following week, the White Citizens' Council reprinted the names in a large advertisement. Reprisals against the Negroes soon took their toll. Within a short time, all but two of the original fifty-three families had withdrawn their names from the petition and these two subsequently left town. Firings and boycotts cut down the petitioners. Even the withdrawal of a name did not mean restoration to a normal way of life.

"I haven't completed a job since my name was on that petition," said Caesar Lloyd, a painter. "I've got a wife and six children, and I'll probably have to leave here soon. . . . I've been borrowing on groceries from a small Negro store here, and borrowing money outright from a colored friend of mine, but I can't afford this any more." [21]

Jasper Mims, a leader in the petition drive, had expected pressure, but had been unprepared for the solid front exhibited by whites. "I'm a carpenter," he said, "and I didn't get any work for a long time, not even from a lot of Negroes, because I was known as the leader of the NAACP and they were afraid of me. . . . I signed that petition because I felt I was working for freedom. I don't feel free now . . . once someone called my wife up and told her that my body had just been found. I removed my name shortly after that." [22]

Nick Roberts, head of the Citizens' Council and a local civic leader, justified the white response by reference to "constitutional government": "You see, that's not the way we do things around here. When someone wants something he goes to a person and asks for it. He doesn't mail a paper and demand it. I'm not surprised . . . that the people don't want to do any business with the Negroes and firing all of them . . . . . our Constitutional government just is not operated for some minority to come in and say 'We Demand.' " [23]

Certainly, the Yazoo City government could not tolerate this request from a minority. The white pressure succeeded in driving many Negroes from town and caused the NAACP membership to dwindle from two hundred to sixty-five. Later attempts at school desegregation met with equal failure. By 1964, the remaining Yazoo City Negroes cowered in fear and stayed in the place assigned to them by the white man. Without economic power or outside assistance, they had no chance of breaking down segregation.

The single time when school barriers collapsed in Mississippi came in 1962 when Governor Ross Barnett, who once had named God as "the original segregationist," forced a showdown with the federal government at the University of Mississippi. The events of this crisis, including the gun battle in which twenty-five marshals were wounded and a French newsman killed, have been so well documented they need no recapitulation here.*

---

* The best objective account of the "Ole Miss" crisis can be found in James Silver's *Mississippi: The Closed Society* and in *The Oxford Disaster: Price of Defiance* by former state representative Karl Wiesenburg.

Mississippi:
The Degrading Society

The stately Wilson House, Grant's headquarters at one point in the Civil War, stands two miles outside of Yazoo City. During the interval before Sherman's and Grant's troops finally joined in the Confederacy's defeat, many Union officers stayed at the house. They scratched various mottoes and inscriptions on the walls. One of the few still legible today serves as perhaps the most just indictment of Mississippi then and in the present conflict. "To the owner of this house," a Union soldier had written, "Your case is a hard one and I pity you."

One hundred years after this judgment had been rendered, Mississippi's case, however refurbished with new slogans, seems equally pitiful. In the name of the doctrine of white supremacy and the unscientific myths of the virtue of racial integrity, Mississippi whites have created a society which has systematically sought the degradation of Negro citizens. By conscious policy, the state's rulers have excluded Negroes from the electoral process; they have intimidated them with a rule of terror, and they have denied Negroes access to a decent education. In creating a permanently inferior class of slaves, the white policy worked. By any statistic one examined, it was apparent that the state's leaders had succeeded in keeping the Negro in a wretchedly subservient position: [24]

—Most Negroes lived in housing unfit for human habitation. The 1960 Census categorized 66 per cent of all Negro housing as "dilapidated or deteriorating." In the rural areas (where a large majority of Negroes subsisted), 71 per cent of the Negro homes had neither toilets nor bathing facilities.

—Proportionately, about one-third more Negroes died each year than whites. In Mississippi, the chances of a Negro baby's dying within the first year of life were twice those of a white child. While health conditions generally improved, the Negro death rate in 1960 was still not as low as the 1913 white death rate.

—According to a report of the state school superintendent, one-half of Negro schools in Mississippi had no equipment whatsoever.

—More than 90 per cent of public libraries in the state denied admittance to Negroes.

—More than 7 per cent of Negroes could not find any employment in 1960, a rate of unemployment twice that of whites.

—In 1960, Negro families had an average annual income of $606, 71 per cent less than that of whites. In rural regions, the average Negro family earned $474. During the decade of the 1950's, rural Negroes actually lost income in relation to whites.

—In response to these conditions, Negroes who had money left Mississippi in droves. Between 1950 and 1960, 315,680 Negroes departed from their home state. These migrants came overwhelmingly from the ranks of younger, better-educated Negroes.

As the year 1964 opened, various forces converged upon Mississippi with the goal of integrating this backward society into twentieth-century America. From the outside, several court decisions stripped away the whites' last legal excuses. In 1962, the Supreme Court reaffirmed that no state may require racial segregation of transportation; in 1963, the court upheld a number of injunctions against discriminating voter registrars; in 1964, Federal courts broke down the last-ditch barriers to school integration in such important counties as Harrison, Leake, and Hinds. A score of new voting discrimination suits entered the courts and some of the worst counties like Sunflower (where in 1963 only 114 out of 13,524 Negroes had been allowed to register) faced the prospect of federal action. And the state, like the nation, awaited the imminent passage of the omnibus Civil Rights bill.

Various private agencies also had increased the pressure on

Mississippi. In 1963, the U.S. Civil Rights Commission urged President Kennedy to drop federal aid to Mississippi if the state did not end its discrimination. This would be a serious blow to a state which received $650 million in federal aid while paying out taxes of only $270 million. During the same year, the Methodist church issued a long overdue statement opposing segregation. Twenty-eight young Methodist ministers in Mississippi upheld the resolution (three were immediately fired). Also in 1963, an "airlift" of food came out of the North to help Leflore County Negroes who had been blocked from federal food shipments by county officers.

All of the movement for change did not come from these so-called "foreign" sources. By 1964, powerful segments within Mississippi society increasingly demanded progress. Signs that neither apathy nor terror had subdued the Negro population appeared throughout the state.

One indication that rebellion stirred within the Negro community was that for the first time in this century four Negroes stood as candidates for national office. They ran under the banner of the Freedom Democratic party, a new political organ designed to challenge the supremacy of Mississippi's regular Democratic machine. In addition to seeking the favor of registered voters, the four candidates launched a "freedom registration" drive. They sought to register as many as possible of Mississippi's 400,000 disenfranchised Negroes upon "freedom registration books." These forms asked the regular questions required under Mississippi law, but did not ask for the various interpretations of the constitution demanded by the state. No one believed that the freedom candidates could triumph over the usual party war-horses, but their candidacy was expected to bring issues to the people of Mississippi, dramatize the atmosphere of voter discrimination, and serve as a basis for challenging the right of the regular state apparatus to continue as a part of the national Democratic party.

Diverse in background—illustrative of the Negro mass move-

ment they personified—the four candidates had in common only
one trait: unusual bravery. The Reverend John Cameron, for example, a thirty-one-year-old minister from Hattiesburg, ran part of
his campaign from jail, after he had been arrested under the state's
antipicketing law. James Houston, a retired seventy-four-year-old
machinist and native of Vicksburg, had suffered arrest as early as
1934, when he participated in a rural meeting called to discuss
New Deal programs. Police arrested him again in 1963 when he
attempted to lead a march from a Jackson Methodist church to the
city hall.

Perhaps the most significant candidate was Mrs. Fannie Lou
Hamer, who ran in the Second Congressional District against Representative Jamie Whitten, then chairman of the powerful House
Appropriations Subcommittee on Agriculture.* Mrs. Hamer, the
wife of a Delta sharecropper, had been raised in a family of twenty
children. She lived in a shack in Sunflower County and knew inti-
mately the sufferings of her fellow Negroes.

As a child, she had dropped out of school to help pick cotton in
the fields and cut corn stalks. Her family had prospered until a
white man, jealous of their success, poisoned their stock.

After her marriage, Mrs. Hamer became increasingly involved
in the civil rights movement. "All my life I've been sick and tired,"
she said in 1964. "Now I'm sick and tired of being sick and
tired. . . . I'm showing people that a Negro can run for office." 25

Her commitment to political activity cost Mrs. Hamer heavily.
The white intimidation began on August 31, 1962, when she and
seventeen others went to the Indianola courthouse to register to
vote. Police stopped the bus and arrested them because, the policeman said, the bus was painted the wrong color. After her release,

* The strategic placement of men like Whitten made it almost impossible
for the federal government to punish some of Mississippi's wrongdoing.
If the Agriculture Department, for example, had tried to stop the misuse
of food surpluses, Whitten could have retaliated by blocking all agricultural
appropriations.

the owner of the plantation where the Hamers worked ordered them to leave.

Mrs. Hamer continued to work for the Negro cause by distributing food to needy families and participating in COFO educational activities. In June of 1963, while returning from a SNCC workshop, she was arrested in Winoma. Along with others, she was incarcerated in the local jail. As Mrs. Hamer recalls the subsequent events, she was carried into a room where a policeman handed a blackjack to a Negro man:

> And the Negro, he said, "This what you want me to use?" The State patrolman said, "That's right, and if you don't use it on her, you know what I'll use on you." [26]

The Negro beat her while police watched:

> And me screamin', it made a plain-clothes man . . . get so hot and worked up and he just run there and started hittin' me on the back of my head. And I was tryin' to guard some of the licks with my hands and they just beat my hands till they turned blue.[27]

The police assigned another Negro to beat her and also to set to work on others who had accompanied Mrs. Hamer:

> They whipped Annette Ponder and I heard her screamin'. After a while she passed by where I was in the cell and her mouth was bleedin' and her hair was standin' up on her head and you know it was horrifyin' . . . After I got out of jail, half dead, I found out that Medgar Evers had been shot down in his own yard.[28]

Mrs. Hamer ran for office in the home district of Senator Eastland, an area where 68 per cent of the people are Negro. Only 1.2 per cent of voting-age Negroes, however, had been allowed to register. The exploitation in Mrs. Hamer's region extended into all areas of life. Most Negroes served as virtual slaves on plantations. Their children attended inferior schools (an average of $60 a pupil was expended in their maintenance), and the schools closed in September and October in order that the children could work in the fields. After the Supreme Court decision of 1954, the state abolished compulsory school attendance. In consequence, many Delta children spent all of their time in the fields. Many Negro children had no clothes to wear at all, except for charity donations coming in from the North.

Mrs. Hamer knew that she had little chance of winning an election, but her campaign served to expose the political, social, and economic discrimination which plagued Delta Negroes. "We been waitin' all our lives," she exclaimed, "and still gettin' killed, still gettin' hung, still gettin' beat to death. Now we're tired waitin'!" [29] Because of her 1963 beating, Mrs. Hamer fell seriously ill during the campaign.

People like Mrs. Hamer did not stand entirely alone for they worked closely with the national civil rights organizations united in COFO. All of COFO's activities—its voting drives, community centers, and freedom schools—had the general aim of preparing Negroes "to challenge the myth of our society, to perceive more clearly its realities and to find . . . new directions for action." [30] On a more tangible level, COFO planned to establish educational facilities, a teen-age work corps, a "tool-loan bank," courses in literacy, practical training in citizenship, and a legal and political advice bureau.

As COFO and the state's Negroes made their plans for the summer, Mississippi's whites developed a counter-strategy. The prospects of a combined assault—an invasion of outsiders, a Negro revolt within the state, and a series of adverse legal decisions—provoked extensive preparations by ruling forces in Mississippi.

On a legal level, state legislators passed a series of bills designed to restrict civil rights activities: a law to allow towns to "lend" fire equipment and personnel to each other to quiet civil disturbances; a bill permitting municipalities to restrict the movement of their citizens; a law against the circulation of pamphlets which encouraged boycotts; and a bill prohibiting picketing when it "interfered" with the "free use of public streets or sidewalks." In March, Governor Paul Johnson called for an increase in the number of highway patrolmen and wide latitude in their use throughout the state. He announced his intention to maintain law and order and his opposition to the "invaders." There was sufficient room in the state prison, he noted, for "overflow prisoners." As he called for greater powers, the governor told the state legislature: "If we allow these invaders to succeed in their dastardly scheme; that is, if we allow them to commit violence or to provoke our own citizens to violence we will be guilty of a very costly error." [31]

Municipal authorities also took action. In Canton, for example, the city council passed a law making it a crime to distribute literature without a city permit. During the month of January, local officials launched a campaign of harassment against civil rights workers already present in the city; police seized a list of names taken from a voter registration petition; a SNCC worker from Ohio was arrested for contributing to the delinquency of a minor by causing a teen-ager to distribute pamphlets of a "libelous nature"; police began to stop automobiles entering or leaving the town; and the city halted operation of all Negro taxicabs, claiming that they possessed faulty permits.

In Jackson, the most populous city in the state, Mayor Allen Thompson built up a small army to combat civil rights "disorders." To defend his city, Mayor Thompson beefed up his police force to 450 men, twice as many as any other city of Jackson's size had. A reserve pool of deputies and citizens' patrols backed up the police force. Calling upon a $2.2 million budget, the Jackson department bought two hundred new shotguns and gave tear-gas masks to every man. Thompson's motorized corps included troop lorries, two half-ton searchlight trucks, and three trailer trucks designed to imprison demonstrators. Two detention compounds, the mayor said, could handle 25,000 prisoners.

"Thompson's Tank" completed the police armament. The tank —a 13,000-pound armored truck, holding twelve men—cost about one dollar a pound. The mayor described it as "a wonderful thing," but the tank failed in its first task of quelling a demonstration at Jackson State College. Protesting the release of a white man who had run down a Negro co-ed, students had poured into the streets. The Mayor ordered the tank into action, but as it pulled up, a tear gas shell exploded inside it, and twelve crying policemen quickly disembarked.

Less respectable white groups also made their counterplans. The Association for the Preservation of the White Race increased its organizational activity and, by May of 1964, claimed 30,000 members. The Ku Klux Klan held open rallies and boasted of 100,000 members. The KKK—attacking the "black Warren court" and scoring the Negro as "too dumb to learn, filthy, diseased and evil-minded"—called for violence, if necessary, and a representative of the National States' Rights party wrote to the chairman of SNCC:

> All race-mixers will some day be brought to justice for their crimes against humanity and all future generations, and, since race-mixing is morally more criminal than murder, it would give me great satisfaction if I were selected to sit on such a jury.
>
> You are right about one thing—this is going to be a long, hot summer—but the "heat" will be applied to the race-mixing TRASH by the *DECENT* people. . . . When your communist-oriented GOONS get to Mississippi, I hope they get their just dues. . . .[32]

As Dixie girded itself for a siege, the first wave of summer volunteers entered Mississippi in June of 1964. They and thousands of Negroes sought to effect a peaceful yet radical change in the southern social structure. Idealistic and energetic, scared and sometimes naïve, the civil rights workers fanned throughout the state. Would they be engulfed in an eruption of violence? Would they somehow make a dent in the walls of prejudice which surrounded the state? No one at this stage could venture a certain prediction. But those who had been battling in the state for many years—Bob Moses and Aaron Henry, Mrs. Hamer and James Silver—were sure of one judgment: that the movement could not be stopped by arrests or bombs, firings or boycotts. A new phase in the Mississippi revolt had been entered and a new spirit had released the Mississippi Negro from his pose of indifference. As the summer began, Fannie Hamer expressed this determination:

"We're tired of all this beatin', we're tired of takin' this. It's been a hundred years and we're still bein' beaten and shot at, crosses are still being burned because we want to vote. But I'm goin' to stay in Mississippi and if they shoot me down, I'll be buried here.[33]

2

The First Wave:
June, 1964

IN the middle of June, several hundred civil rights workers headed for the hills around Carthage, the snake-filled swamps in the East, and for the Delta region, where bleakly isolated shacks floated in an ocean of cotton. A few "professionals" moved toward the Southwest, a place of dangerous repute since five Negroes had recently been killed there and whites had armed themselves with machine guns and hand grenades.

Many of the new workers checked in at COFO headquarters in Jackson, a one-story, white plaster building, squeezed between a tavern and an unkempt cemetery. From there, Bob Moses and a small regular staff coordinated the freedom schools and mass meetings, the community centers and canvassing activities in the state. The headquarters had an air of disorganized bustle. Its cardboard interior walls were covered with posters, clippings, and news bulletins ("Hattiesburg: Church Burned to the Ground"; "Ruleville:

4 CR Workers Arrested"). Another wall had security instructions ("Be careful at Steven's Kitchen. Negro informers are reporting overheard conversations"). One wall, titled "The Opposition," displayed a picture of the Grand Wizard of the Klan, and quotes from local newspapers. The telephones rang constantly as reports came into the office, sometimes calling for lawyers to aid a beleaguered post in Greenwood or Canton, Itta Bena or SoSo. In the evening, two or three guitarists would lounge on the rickety couches at the front of the office, singing quiet, plaintive freedom songs.

The full-time workers, old-timers drawn from SNCC and CORE, moved in and out, on their way to other towns. Clad in dungarees, these people lived on subsistence pay (food, lodging, and nine dollars a week). They worked a sixteen-hour day and had often submitted to arrest. Although young, averaging twenty-three years in age, the professional workers had a stoical air and seldom smiled. They made a fetish of using the most monotonous tones to describe the dangers which faced them. Like an infantry unit that had survived many skirmishes, they repeated obscure "inside jokes" and exhibited a slight disdain for newcomers moving into their ranks. Their premature air of cynicism did not suit their young faces but served them well in the state's jails.

Bob Moses described some of the workers as very bitter about their experience and, particularly, at the nation's previous lack of interest in the movement. "We ourselves have been working in Mississippi for the last three years," Moses said. "So we have asked people to come in and share that risk."

The volunteers who elected to join the Mississippi project got a complete briefing on the perils which confronted them. At a training session in Oxford, Ohio, the veteran staff taught workers how to protect themselves from beatings and informed them about the nature of southern customs and justice. James Forman, the burly national leader of SNCC, led their education. A man of 200 pounds, Forman had developed a remarkable ability to keep his own temper under control. When he warned one audience at the orientation that "I may be killed, you may be killed, the whole staff may go," his words carried authority.[1]

Such warnings were repeated many times at Oxford. Another worker, Willie Peacock, told the volunteers of a beating he had received after a traffic violation arrest. "When you go down those cold stairs at the police station," he told them, "you don't know if you're going to come back or not. You don't know if you can take those licks without fighting, because you might decide to fight back. It all depends on how you want to die.

" 'Nigger,' the man told me, 'do you believe I'd just as soon kill you as look at you?' I says yes, but not fast enough: Whack!—up comes his left hand! 'I'm going to erase every data of doubt from your mind,' he says. 'Ain't the white people been good to you, ain't they taken good care of you?' He wanted me to crawl and all that bull jazz. I'd have killed him, the things he was calling me, but I never could have gotten away." [2]

Seminar leaders at Oxford cautioned the volunteers about ways to keep out of difficulty in the South: Certain counties like Amite had to be avoided at all costs; driving with a Negro in an integrated car at night was forbidden; if caught in a violent mob, one should crouch with knees up to protect the belly and with arms wrapped around the head. COFO leaders told three-man teams to keep in touch by telephone each night; if one man disappeared, the others could inform the local office.

Such advice may have seemed melodramatic, like a rerun of an old movie about the European resistance to Nazism. Yet, at one point during the briefing sessions when the volunteers seemed not to take the potential danger seriously, a veteran of Mississippi exploded: "Ask Jimmy over there what he thinks about Mississippi. He has six slugs in him, man, and the last one went right through the back of his neck when he was driving a car outside Greenwood." He pointed to thin ascetic Jesse Harris. "Ask Jesse here, he's been beaten so we couldn't rcognize him, time and time and time and time again. If you don't get scared, pack up and get

the hell out of here, because we don't need any people who don't
know what they're doing here." [3]

The screening process for volunteers had been rigorous. From
Stanford University, only 45 of an original 300 applicants eventually got to Mississippi, and at Wesleyan University half of the
students who wished to participate were not admitted. Some "beatnick" types inevitably appeared on the scene, as well as a handful
of existentialists talking vaguely of "commitment." On the whole,
the students were a cross-section of the strawberry-and-cream All-
American youth found on northern campuses. Professor John
Maguire of Wesleyan succinctly stated the criteria for rejecting
certain applicants:

> We are largely worried about two types: those who are looking
> for a new kind of "kick," sexual or otherwise; and those evangel-
> ical souls who will arrive in Mississippi with no more understand-
> ing of the situation than to turn their eyes skyward and say,
> "Lord, here I am." [4]

The final group of volunteers, composed mostly of college
youth, contained the religious and the revolutionary, the sons of
congressmen and labor leaders, white and black. "The surprising
thing is the fact that there aren't more beatnicks," said Dr. Joseph
Brenner, an M.I.T. psychiatrist who helped in the selection
process. "They're an extraordinarily healthy bunch of kids,
mentally and physically. There aren't a lot of starry-eyed idealists
here." [5]

After the staging in Oxford, the volunteers slipped off in carloads to their positions in the South. Their arrival sparked an
outpouring of abuse from white spokesmen. "What we are wit-
nessing makes me want to vomit," editorialized George Keith in
The Carthaginian, "a dozen misguided children arrived in our
county Tuesday. . . . It is absolutely sickening to see the freakish
people as they mingle with the Negro." * [6]

---

* Soon after expressing this view, Mr. Keith visited the Carthage volunteers and asked their opinion of his editorial. When told it was libelous,
Keith looked surprised. He apparently believed he had helped the cause of

A Jackson columnist by the name of Jimmy Ward, approving the closing of an integrated public park, declared: "Forced race-mixing in other cities has produced neighborhood conditions that foster rape, muggings and assaults. Jackson is not immune. . . . You're seeing the first signs of deterioration." [7] He blamed the deterioration on civil rights laws and "beatnick" workers who could use a dose of soap and water.

Senator James Eastland, in his ripest form, brandished an address book taken from an arrested worker, citing it as proof that Communists led the civil rights movement. Jackson newspapers echoed his view, "Experts generally agree that this invasion is a natural for Red infiltration." [8] Senator James Stennis raised the specter of northern intervention when banner headlines in Jackson reported. "Army occupation of state feared. Stennis sees agitator invasion paving way." [9] Senator Richard Russell of Georgia entered the fray by declaring that a "burgeoning bureaucracy" had organized "invasion after invasion of the South." This same Washington bureaucracy had, in his opinion, set off the latest venture, "the greatest crusade since the children's crusade of the middle ages." [10]

The whites used about every epithet found in the pungent Mississippi vocabulary, but they seldom came face to face with these supposedly sinister invaders. The great majority of volunteers settled in Negro homes and were absorbed into a community which the whites had consciously insulated. What, in fact, was the nature of these latter-day invaders of the South?

The Invaders: "Chastened Idealists"

"Hell, all I want is an easy job, a life with no work," Alvin Packer, a seventeen-year-old Negro boy told me. "I've got me a moderation by advising the locals not to inflict bodily harm on "these poor children or the local trash that associates with them."

little cabin spotted on a hill near Charleston. The Union army passed through there and shelled the Southerners. It has a grand view and none of them whites will come up to bother me. They're still afraid of the cannon balls stuck in the dirt. I'll just sit there and laugh at them, once I can make it there."

I met Packer, a boy with a ready smile and a straw hat cocked jauntily over an ear, at the "Freedom House" in Canton. Along with neighborhood teen-agers, he was grinding out mimeographed announcements of a voters' rally. That evening we drove over to a Canton church to distribute the leaflets. The building had recently been rebuilt after a bombing attack. Jagged holes still remained in the stained glass window. With a touch of youthful pride, Packer posed next to the windows for his picture to be taken. On first acquaintance, the boy might have passed for the carefree loafer which he claimed to be. Quickly, however, one detected an unusual sense of purpose underneath his debonair façade.

During three years in Mississippi, the boy had been arrested twenty-eight times on a variety of trumped-up charges. "I'm shooting for the top mark," he said laughingly, "I'm still young and I may break the record." One civil rights worker held the championship with fifty-three arrests.

Packer, a native of New Mexico, came to Mississippi in 1961 to visit relatives. His grandmother had died and had left him a small piece of farm property. At the age of fourteen, he had hoped to farm the land and prosper as his ancestors had. Participation in the Negro liberation movement had been far from his mind.

Like so many of the civil rights workers, young or old, Packer found it difficult to explain why he had joined the movement. "I don't know what started me. I was given a real home here. And then, when I began to understand the people, I learned how they suffered here and what caused it." By chance he met Laurence Guyot, a veteran worker who drew him toward the movement and introduced him to the day-to-day problems of persuading older people to seek their voting rights. Perhaps Packer's experience with some Catholic priests in Mississippi may also have influenced him. He had been raised as a Catholic, wore a cross around his neck for divine protection, and had naturally sought to worship in the Catholic church nearest his home—as it happened, a white one. Breaking the custom of most Mississippi priests, the pastor turned Packer away, embittering the boy. He vowed to change the church and, indeed, two years later, at the order of a local bishop, he gained admittance to the parish. "Before it was against the religion of that priest to let me in," the boy recalled. "Then the Bishop telephoned him and that same priest changed his religion right quickly. Overnight he changed, you might say."

In spite of his youth, Alvin Packer fully committed himself to civil rights work and participated in almost every aspect of it. In 1961, he served as one of the original "Freedom Riders" desegregating the bus-lines. He had received a beating for that in McComb. In 1962, he switched to voter registration. In Hattiesburg, after helping to bring out four hundred people to attempt to register, he braved the water hoses which the police used to disperse protesters. Later, he helped organize the Mississippi Student Union, a group of 1,500 youths dedicated to bettering the Negro's condition.

Perhaps because of his insouciant manner, COFO leaders sometimes chose the boy to act as a trouble shooter in the tougher towns. He worked briefly in Neshoba County (later to become famous because of its capital, Philadelphia) and in the equally nasty town of Leland. There, in February of 1964, he made the mistake of wearing a SNCC button which showed white and Negro hands clasped in friendship. Two carloads of whites chased him out of Leland, yelling, "Run, nigger, run!" He found shelter for the night under a bridge. In March, while driving a car loaded with books for a freedom school, he was stopped by police near Leland for passing out subversive literature. (The books included an encyclopedia, a set of "Oz" volumes, and copies of the American Constitution.)

On a similar errand of supplying books to a freedom school, he was taken in by the Holly Springs police. The town had long been viewed as a dangerous place by civil rights workers. For fourteen hours in the city jail, Alvin Packer learned the reason. "They had arrested me with books in the car," he remembered. "They told me I was trying to overthrow the government. Me. Alvin! They asked me if I was James Meredith's brother, doing what I was doing." Unsatisfied with his answers, guards put him in a jail which for Alvin—a well-read, if technically untrained boy—reminded him of old England's Bedlam. "They put me in a hole in the ground. I went down the ladder into a pit. It was real, real dark there. Something like being stuffed in a box."

He remembered the jailer laughing at him and yelling, "Come out of there, Alvin, come on out." The boy did not answer. After his eyes had grown accustomed to the dark, he discovered that the previous inmate had left some canned food, water, and most importantly, a sawed-off broom stick. Later, the boy did not know how long, a jailer opened the top of the pit and peered down. Packer picked up his broom stick when the guard started to climb down. "Come down, come on down," the boy taunted, "We'll see if you is tougher. It's nice and dark down here." The jailer retreated muttering threats about cutting off the boy's food. A COFO lawyer arrived the next day and secured the boy's release on bail.

"Of course, all the jails aren't like that," he quickly added. "Some are plenty nice—good food, good bed, and quiet. The best jail in the state is a federal one. I suppose I'll try that sometime." He sat on a table, relaxed, smiling, reassuring his listeners, and, without quite intending it, telling them that no jail could stop him.

When I met Packer I wondered whether his penalty of imprisonments had been repaid with changes in Mississippi. "Sure, I've seen some progress," he said, mentioning the seemingly little advances which mean a great deal in the South. "There aren't many more of the 'white only' signs around. There are a few Negro policemen, although they sure can't arrest a white man. They changed the name of the police truck in Greenwood. They don't call it 'Niggerbus' no more." He paused when I asked him if there were any changes that had affected all Negroes in Mississippi. "The main thing," he said, "is that most Negroes now believe in their rights and they aren't as afraid of the whites. The old ones might be different. It used to be the old ladies who complained the most in private. Now, they've gotten scared and a few of them even tell their white ladies that they are 'satisfied.' "

I left him in Canton and crossed his tracks once in a while afterwards. He did not look forward to the summer's end. A white policeman had asked him, "You got your nigger-lovers here now but what about later? What are you going to do then when we get all you nigger bucks?" Packer had no answer. He talked vaguely of going to college ("but I don't want to be no preacher or lawyer; they have too many puzzles to solve").

Mostly, I assume, he dreamed of his cabin on the hill, an earthly paradise which he seemed most unlikely to attain.

Except for southern ancestry, Miss Lela Smith of New York had little in common with Alvin Packer. A tall, white, pretty career woman, Miss Smith came from a Quaker community in Virginia, had attended a boarding school and fashionable Goucher College. She had been on *The New Yorker* staff, doing research for articles on fashion and society. She had taken a leave of absence from the Women's International League for Peace and Freedom, where she currently worked as an organizer, in order to spend the summer in Mississippi. She taught English and citizenship in freedom schools in several towns. When I met her, she had just been assigned to Laurel, a dangerous little town which occasionally erupted in riots.

She was quite aware of the potentiality for violence in the Laurel situation. "The first worker down here," she recalled, "was beaten and held incommunicado. He was arrested nine times.

Now, both the whites and Negroes openly display their shotguns. This is the last chance for nonviolence to work in this town."

My job had been to drive her into the Laurel territory. While we telephoned several contacts, we drank some beers in the local café and had a chance to talk. It became apparent that Miss Smith believed that only a nonviolent approach could solve the South's social problems. In the midst of violence, she held to a Gandhian philosophy which she believed would conquer the most grizzled of white "crackers." Her commitment to nonviolence came from her college days. "A boy had invited me to a circus in New York," she remembered. "On the way we heard some soap-box orators for the 'ban the bomb' movement. Their arguments impressed me and since then I have been caught up in a three-ring circus of pacifism." A visit to India in 1959 reinforced her philosophy and led her to a career in pacifist work.

As a Southerner (her family had lived in Virginia since the Revolution and had transported fleeing slaves during the Underground Railway days), Miss Smith knew the difficulties involved in reforming Mississippi. "I was brought up in the rural sections of Virginia," she said. "I know the underlying bitterness of the Negroes. One summer will not change that, but a start can be made, particularly with the women." Perhaps naïvely, Miss Smith particularly hoped to reach white women and, perhaps, to organize a protest movement similar to the "Black Sash" club in South Africa. She felt that the burden of guilt in the South fell not so much on the ignorant, hard-core segregationists but rather on the liberals who had not stood up for Negro rights. "If we liberal Southerners had resisted before, this situation would not have reached such a desperate turn."

Through the summer Miss Smith worked with Negro children in Laurel, trying to put her philosophy into practice. She, like all the volunteers, felt the pressure of being continually watched by hostile whites. "This place reminds me of Albert Camus' *The Plague*," she said. "Everyone, white and black, is infected with fear and hatred. We all feel it. The whites are as fearful as the Negroes. When policemen make arrests here, their hands tremble while holding a gun."

One could feel the same atmosphere of fear in Hattiesburg, a town near Laurel. Police cars prowled in the street in front of COFO headquarters while police officers cast malevolent looks around them. In the first days after a freedom school opened in Hattiesburg, the whites retaliated by slapping workers on the street and shooting into cars. One night, as a visiting rabbi walked a dark street, some whites jumped on him and beat him with lead pipes.

Among the first invaders of Hattiesburg was a tall, dark Negro from Detroit, Arthur Reese. He and his wife, both professional teachers, had been charged with establishing freedom schools in Hattiesburg. Because SNCC workers had been active in this town, the Negro population had pitched into the task eagerly. The Negroes donated books and supplies, and converted their churches to house freedom schools. Even a few whites helped out. One white student, raised in the reactionary classrooms of the University of Southern Mississippi, Hattiesburg's place of higher learning, joined the movement on a full-time basis.

Despite the initial enthusiasm, Reese had expected only about fifty high school students to participate actively in the school. Instead, on the day that Reese opened the school doors, 550 people aged eight to eighty-two registered as students. Reese had to provide courses on everything from sewing to Negro history. "The response overwhelmed us," Reese said. "I suppose people are getting more courage. They know that the white attacks will continue, but they think that only by uniting will they eventually defeat it. And of course, the younger people here badgered the older ones. I saw eleven-year-olds urging their parents to take a stand. Sometimes, circumstances compel involvement. Many people here have lost their jobs or seen their children arrested. They have nothing else to lose."

Reese pulled together a staff of volunteers and professional teachers, put them to work in morning and evening sessions, and found them housing and food in the Negro community. His teachers ranged from youngsters to Professors Otis Pease of Stanford and William Doyle of Chabot College who taught such subjects as the history of Reconstruction. Reese did his job extremely well. He had to advise teachers ("Should they encourage the students to say 'Ma'am'?"), transport students from place to place, and wheedle supplies out of the Jackson headquarters. A typical minor emergency occurred when a typing course had been announced, but no machines could be found; Reese solved it by requisitioning some from local people. Sometimes, Reese served as a makeshift lawyer in extricating his teachers from jail. Robert Beech, a minister who acted as a spiritual adviser to volunteers, had been put in jail for supposedly overdrawing his bank account by seventy dollars. Actually, the bank had refused to honor a deposit which Beech had drawn from an eastern bank. Police released Beech only when Reese and the other project leaders had raised $1,500.

Watching Reese grapple with the problems of running a freedom school, I wondered why he had chosen to spend his summer in Mississippi's turgid atmosphere. "I can't really give a single reason," he said. "Usually, my wife and I escape the 'Negro problem' by taking a vacation in Canada. This year we couldn't . . . you just can't go on teaching, preaching, talking forever, and not doing anything. Being in this terrible situation has changed me. Never before have I had such good friendships with whites, or for that matter, with southern Negroes. We've all had to become adjusted to different cultures. We've had to be understanding friends like never before."

Barney Frank, a graduate student in political science, had Reese's conviction that working in the movement's interracial environment was uniquely enlightening. "It's so rare to function in an atmosphere of total integration," said Frank, who had been assigned to COFO's Jackson headquarters. "It's not just that the barriers of race are down. Here, distinctions of class, age, or religion don't matter either. You can see a young Negro girl giving orders to an elderly white man in the office and nobody thinks twice about it. We're all in this together. The person with greater knowledge of the situation is the one in authority."

Barney Frank, a cigar-chewing, heavy-set man from Bayonne, New Jersey, looked like a politician, precisely the role which he played on the COFO staff. Barney's job was to help organize the Freedom Democratic party, and eventually in August, to lead the party in challenging the regular Democrats. His task was hardly easy. He had to mobilize at least 100,000 people behind the new party and simultaneously fight against the local politicians. At times, this involved him in dangerous work. In early July, for example, police in Canton stopped a truck which carried Freedom Democratic literature. They imprisoned its drivers, pistol-whipped one of them, and impounded the truck. After receiving a coded emergency call on the WATS line—an extended telephone system which allowed every civil rights outpost to communicate with Jackson—Barney Frank set out to retrieve the truck. Since it contained a number of registration forms filled out by local Negroes, it was imperative to get the truck out of police hands. Although at first the police and city attorney denied knowledge of the truck, Frank found it and drove it by night to its destination in northern Mississippi.

While sojourns of this type could have resulted in arrests and beatings, Frank more often found himself embroiled in comic-opera duels with state officials. In order to comply with the state law, for example, Frank had to organize formal precinct meetings in as many counties as possible. When he applied at the state capitol for precinct maps to plot the location of the meetings, a clerk inquired about his purpose.

"I'm forming a new party," he replied.

"Oh, I see," the clerk said with a smile and a wink, "for Governor Wallace of Alabama, I presume ?"

"No, a bit to the left of him," said Frank as he collected the maps.

When precinct meetings and county conventions had been held, Frank called on the secretary of state to register the party officially and to secure copies of the state constitution for distribution to party members. His suspicions aroused by news of the Freedom Democrats, the secretary of state replied that he could not give out the constitution (a strange response in a state that requires its citizens to interpret the document). As for registering the party, the official informed Frank that since he had to rule on the party's status, he could not release any information.

"As secretary of state, I have to decide whether your party is legal or not. It would be a violation of my unbiased judicial standing to give you any advice about organizing the party."

"But all I want to know," said Frank, "is what your requirements are about the forms we should submit. When is our application due?"

"Sorry, but I cannot give you that information."

Frank told the secretary of state that the Freedom Democrats had already been organized and precinct meetings held. Flustered at this news, the secretary of state dropped his judicial composure. "Listen, son," he told Frank, "I've turned down many parties in my day and I'll do it again!" *

Barney Frank had the background to cope with such frustrations. He had attended Harvard College and, after his father's death, had managed a family trucking firm in one of the rougher sections of New Jersey. In an effort to counter Communist accusations against America, he had attended the Helsinki Youth Festival. Young American Communists accused him of being a stool pigeon. "They called me a State Department fink," he recalled, "but I preferred being a fink to a pink." At the time of his inauguration into Mississippi politics, Frank was finishing his doc-

* In July, the secretary of state refused to register the party and called it illegal. He refused to state any grounds for his decision. The decision, well-publicized in the state, led some Negroes to the belief that participation in the party was a crime.

torate at Harvard.

While he worked hard for the Negro cause in Mississippi, Frank did not fall prey to utopian illusions: "This ideology of non-violence is fine, but when it comes to defending my home, I side with those who keep a rifle by the door." As for the future, he did not believe that Negro progress would usher in a millennium. "As conditions improve—and they will—the Negro will seek his spot in suburbia, drink his beer, and watch TV. That's fine! Some of these people think that they are going to reform our entire civilization and that the Negro will be the spearhead of this new age. Not me. I'm not here to build a perfect society, just to insure that the Negro gets a chance to live his life in his own way. If these liberals have the same illusions about the Negro that they used to hold about unions, they are bound for the same disappointment they had in the thirties."

With a good humor which never failed him, Frank turned away any insinuation that his political work could be motivated by idealism. "My reason for coming here? I suppose its just the *reductio ad absurdum* of giving to the Red Cross." He often disparaged the importance of his own work: "The movement is really one of chastened idealism. We're not making a 100 per cent commitment to what is a very tough fight the year around." However much he played down his own importance, Frank's work seemed quite significant to me when I last saw him standing night guard at a Vicksburg freedom school. The school was scheduled to be bombed that night and Frank, despite his protestations of cynicism, had been one of the few who volunteered to guard it against attackers.

These "chastened idealists" were the invaders of Mississippi. Young and old, Catholic and Quaker and Jew, dedicated to non-violence or desiring simply to give reality to the American dream, they came from all parts of the United States to storm the fortress of segregation. They had been told before their departure that the Justice Department of the national government could do nothing to protect them. And even their friends in the North warned them that they might be little more than sacrificial lambs. "It is a dreadful thing to say, but it needs saying," wrote columnist Joseph Alsop. "The organizers who sent these young people into Mississippi must have wanted, even hoped for, martyrs." [11]

The invaders had, in fact, entered into an undeclared guerrilla war, one which would take its martyrs and produce its unique heroes. The question remained whether martyrdom would be enough to overcome the organized terrorist movement dedicated to white supremacy in Mississippi.

Probing Operations

The invaders moved into the countryside where Union soldiers had once marched. Almost everywhere the newcomers went, Negroes met them with warmth and grace, although at times their greeting was tempered by fear. The dispersion of power within a town, the unity and economic independence of its Negro population, the ruthlessness of white repression—these were the factors which affected the welcome accorded to civil rights workers. The initial moves made by the invaders depended upon the sophistication of the local Negroes and the extent of white terrorism.

The experience of three areas, Ruleville, Moss Point, and Clarksdale, illustrates the successes and failures of the invaders in quite diverse communities.

Ruleville typified the sun-drenched, cotton-rich Delta towns which civil rights workers infiltrated. Mayor Charles Durrough had governed Ruleville since 1952. The mayor distributed Citizens' Council literature from city hall and led the dominant white minority in the town. He expressed his attitude toward the United States Constitution when he told a civil rights worker, "That law has not come here yet." Senator James Eastland, the powerful head of the Senate Judiciary Committee, lived in Ruleville and had an office on the second floor of the Bank of Ruleville. As Mississippi's top politician, he told the Senate in 1946, "I assert that the Negro race is an inferior race. The doctrine of white supremacy is one which, if adhered to, will save America."

Eastland's home town drew its parched living from cotton, corn, rice, and soybeans. While the white people enjoyed an average family income of $2,000, the average Negro family earned $600. The town's population fell into three fairly distinct groups. The "white Americans," personified by Eastland and Durrough, dominated the city and the agricultural economy which supported it. A large group of "white foreigners"—Jews, Italians, and Chinese— served as merchants but seldom as members of the Ruleville social elite. Negroes found it easier to talk with the "foreigners" who, they reported, were seldom involved directly in attacking Negroes.

Civil rights workers had hoped to make contact with the foreign element in Ruleville, but the first attempts in June met with rebuffs. Occupied with proving its own status, the foreign group tried to dissociate itself from Negroes. "What do you think about all this nigger stuff?" one Chinese merchant in Ruleville asked me, accenting his words in a strange combination of Cantonese and Southern American. "They are just a bunch of little children. We can't let children vote, now can we?" Some Negroes stood at the cash register next to the merchant as he talked, but their faces showed no signs of emotion. Later, outside the store, they came up, clasped my hand, and told me of their desire to vote.

The Negroes in Ruleville divided into two sections: the "Sanctified Quarter" Negroes (who received their name from a neighborhood church) and the "Compress Quarter" community (a relatively prosperous group taking its name from a cotton gin at the edge of the city). The "Compress" Negroes, like the Negro middle class throughout the South, had close economic ties to the *status quo* and hesitated to challenge it openly.

The "Sanctified" Negroes, led by Mrs. Fannie Hamer, were usually impoverished, unemployed people. Despite reprisals, the

"Sanctified" Negroes provided the most militant civil rights workers and had organized the "Ruleville Citizenship Club," a spearhead for voters' activities. "The people here have been through the mill," a volunteer reported at Jackson, "and physical violence is no stranger to their streets. Literally thousands of pounds of food and clothing have been distributed from sources up North because the whites have cut off all relief." The intimidation had not prevented the registration of twenty-nine voters. "None of them will turn back," the reporter said.

These voters took the lead in the Citizenship Club. In February of 1964, the club rented buses and carried about four hundred persons to Indianola in a vain attempt at registration. Club members gave housing to forty white volunteers "despite the fact that Mayor Durrough personally made a house-to-house canvass warning Negroes . . . and despite the fact that they have every reason to expect economic reprisal." [12]

While the poorer Negroes greeted the volunteers warmly, the white community, including its churches, built a wall of hostility. On June 28, for example, the Reverend James Corson, minister of the Methodist Wesley Foundation at Stanford University, attempted to attend a white church service. Corson, a white man, said that Mayor Charles Durrough advised him, "You've come down here to live with Negroes, so you can go to church with them." The mayor told Corson and three other white workers that he would personally get them to leave if they attended a white church. That Sunday the four received a kind welcome at one of Ruleville's Negro churches.

The incoming civil rights workers made few other attempts to reach the white community. Instead, they concentrated their effort on establishing a freedom school and intensifying the drive for voters. Each night in June they held mass meetings at a Baptist church, Williams Chapel. About one hundred people attended every night. As the meetings generated enthusiasm in the Negro community, the whites retaliated.

On June 23, a car of white men chased reporters out of town at 85 m.p.h.

On June 24, roving cars damaged nine Negro homes with bottles thrown from cars. Unidentified people fired shotguns at the homes of Ruleville's most active Negro voters.

On June 25, someone tried to burn down Williams Chapel by starting a fire with seven bags soaked with gasoline. Local officials charged that Negroes had started the fire themselves.

Each day brought an incident of one kind or another. Even though some Negroes lost their jobs for housing white workers, the movement seemed to win the allegiance of an increasing number of Negroes. The day after the church was burned, for example, nine Negroes went to Indianola to try to register (two of them had tried twelve times before).

The Ruleville contingent also had the job of opening up nearby rural areas which had not yet been touched by civil rights activity. This was a hard task, for they faced both white opposition and the lethargy ingrained into plantation Negroes after years of submitting to the system. Two workers (Len Edwards, a law student and son of a California congressman, and Joe Smith, a sophomore from Wesleyan) had to make the first contacts with Drew, a little town near Ruleville.[13] When they arrived in Drew on June 24, a police car immediately began to tail them. Their calls on Negroes often proved fruitless, for too often, as the Negroes watched the police car drifting by, they said that they were not interested in voting.

Edwards and Smith kept working in Drew and soon results began to show. By the end of June, a few Drew people secretly attended rallies in Ruleville. A few weeks later, the citizens of Drew staged a full-scale voters' meeting of their own. Although police arrested ten women and fifteen men who attended the meeting—and the superintendent of the county farm told a lawyer that he would not be responsible for the prisoners' safety—it had become clear that the area around Ruleville had undergone a profound change.

Moss Point, a sultry town on the Gulf Coast several hundred miles southeast of Ruleville, had never been a focus of civil rights agitation. COFO leaders, on the urging of local NAACP officials, decided to send a first contingent to the area in June. Two Negroes and two whites, Charles Green, Howard Kirschenbaum, Ron Ridenour, and Fred Meely, arrived in the city on June 21. They met with Negro leaders at a local café and heard how the police had threatened to close businesses of Negroes who participated in civil rights work, how people had been run from town for speaking out about burnings and beatings, and how Negro informers served on the city's staff. Negro families earned about one-fourth the usual white income, one-eighth of the national average income. The voting situation, however, seemed to offer good prospects: 24 per cent of the Negro population had registered and three out of five eligible people who approached the registrar succeeded in getting their names on the books. The COFO workers decided to concentrate their first efforts on increasing the flow of registered voters.

In a few days the workers had made extensive contacts within the Negro community, had been invited to stay in some houses, had equipped an office, and had even started building a 5,000-book library. They announced a voters' rally to be held on July 1 in a local park and they commenced door-to-door canvassing of potential voters. While the initial reception had been heartening, the white police also planned its special form of welcome.

On the night of June 30, two of the white COFO workers attended an NAACP meeting and then headed for a local café. There they met with some Negro leaders. As one worker later reported to Jackson, "I was told by community people about whites throwing poisoned candy and gum around the town. Two small children were supposed to have been poisoned badly." The worker left the café and sat on a lawn. He saw a policeman approaching. The officer said, "What are you doing here, boy?"

After a few minutes of talking, the boy was arrested for investigation and sped at 85 m.p.h. to the Moss Point jail. Highway Patrol officers, Pascagoula and Moss Point police, and sheriff's deputies awaited him at the jail.

"We treat our niggers well here," one policeman told the COFO volunteer. "We don't want you Commie outside agitators coming in—people get killed for less." Another policeman, tapping his billy in his hand, added, "You boys are in for a good whipping."

The white worker and another arrested volunteer were placed in the jail's "nigger bull-pen," a most unusual occurrence. The jailer told Negro inmates, "Here they are, get 'em boys!" As the worker laconically put it in his report, the Negroes "were not moved to beat us." Fifteen minutes later, the police transferred the boys to a white section of the jail. As one of the volunteers remembered the incident: "This was about 12:30 A.M., Wednesday. At the white cell, the officers tried to incite white prisoners to take out their aggression on the volunteers—'It's whipping time.' " [14] A white prisoner commented that he hated all niggers and nigger-lovers and that "COFOers" were there to be beaten by whites (as they had been in several other jails). Somehow the prisoners could not decide who should whip the boys. One worker, Ron Ridenour spoke to a Mexican prisoner in Spanish, letting a little tension out of the situation. For three hours, as the civil rights workers lay on the floor, the other inmates argued whether it would be wise to beat them.

Early in the morning, police officers entered the cell. They took the workers to a finger-printing desk where police tried to scare them by telling atrocity stories about the project leader having been found cut in half and about a girl worker who had been brutally raped. After twelve hours in jail, the workers were released. Legal redress could not be won since Mississippi law allows police to hold people for seventy-two hours without a charge.

As the month proceeded, the civil rights workers continued to press their activity with potential voters. Evening meetings and house canvassing by local teen-agers stirred enthusiasm in the Negro community. Although five men lost their jobs for housing white workers and the Knights of Pythias Hall, a center of voter meetings, was firebombed, the COFO staff escorted a steady number of voter applicants to the city hall. On one typical day, fifty local Negroes lined up to register. By evening, thirty-three had not been let into the building, ten people "failed" the voting test, and only seven had become voters. Blocked from participation in the usual electoral process, 1,900 Negroes had filled out "freedom registration" forms by the end of the month.

The white community did its best to frighten workers and Moss Point Negroes. Threatening telephone calls kept the COFO office busy and unmarked cars cruised constantly around the houses where workers slept. At the courthouse, one civil rights volunteer said, an ex-sheriff intimidated potential voters by warning, "Just lift your hand at me. I just want you to lift your hand at me, I'd like to blow your head off." In early July, the local grand jury subpoenaed a number of Negroes to inquire about COFO's "subversive" activities.

The threats often fulfilled their purpose. Parents hesitated to send their children to the newly established freedom school and the number of voter applicants dwindled as the month went on. The height of repression in Moss Point came one evening early in July at a voter's rally. Three hundred Negroes had gathered to hear Laurence Guyot, SNCC project director for the area. At the end of the meeting, while the audience sang "We Shall Overcome," four white men in a passing car fired two bursts of bullets into the hall. Jessie Mae Stalworth, a Moss Point Negro woman, fell with several bullets in her; two other women sustained minor injuries.

Later in the evening, two Negro cars pursued an automobile they believed had been involved in the shooting. When they finally stopped the car, one of the Negroes got out. He found a shotgun aimed at him by whites, turned back to his car, and discovered that police were ready to haul it away. The police put him in a state highway patrol car, drove to the Pascagoula jail, and charged him with attempted assault. The police made no attempt to search the white car.

The shooting divided the Negro community into two camps. For some Negroes, the assault inspired a spirit of resistance. The following night, five hundred people turned out for a rally, eighty volunteered to do voter canvassing, and twenty-eight donated their cars to the movement. The majority of Moss Point Negroes, however, were frightened by the attack and tended to withdraw from the movement. The swift use of violence in a town where civil rights work had just begun served to deter many Negroes from seeking their rights.

Setbacks, such as those at Moss Point, inevitably occurred during the first groping weeks of the campaign. In general, however, the movement made impressive progress. Clarksdale, a small, hot town in northern Mississippi, presents a typical example of a successful project. Challenged by the leadership of Aaron Henry, a local druggist and perhaps the most able Negro leader in the state, the Clarksdale Negroes united in common cause. By the beginning of July, they had already built an excellent library, established a "Freedom House" in the middle of town, and opened a freedom school.

The school enrolled students from junior high-school age through the college years. The pupils studied a range of subjects from typing (the most popular course) to Spanish (taught to a single energetic teen-ager by an expert from California). An air of free discussion, so new to southern Negroes, pervaded the school and this, above all, seemed to stimulate the students. When asked to write an essay on Mississippi, for example, the students used the occasion to vent their antagonism toward the state. One twelve-year-old boy wrote:

> Life in Mississippi is very hard and cruel. The people can't vote, go to school, go to a public place, such as parks, restaurants, hospitals, and hotels. On the subject of law, there is no such

thing as justice for Negroes. The Negro people are persecuted, intimidated, and blamed for all crimes that are committed.

The Negro lives in a shack not fit for a dog. I pray that a big
wind storm do not come, for their will be no shack for the Negro
to live and their surely will be death.

So God please set my people free.

A fifteen-year-old boy wrote about his home state:

Many say Mississippi is a bad place to live. Well it is, if you
hate going to the back of a street car, if you hate using the back
door to a restaurant, and hate to hear a white call your parents
girl and boy . . . if you hate all these things and many others,
I join you in saying then Mississippi is the worst state to live in.

These embittered youngsters supplemented their schooling with
active political work in Clarksdale. They, together with COFO
volunteers, brought a stream of applicants to the voter registrar's
office. At times, particularly in rural areas or the less educated
sections of town, the volunteers found that a barrier of fear and
unlettered apathy confronted them.

Hounded by years of terror, Negroes sometimes met the offers
of white workers with unbelief or even suspicion. In the deterio-
rated Riverton section, for example, Stanford student Robert Newberry conducted the canvassing. In a not uncommon exchange, he
talked with an old Negro. "I'm Bob Newberry," he said, "and we
have a project this summer, helping people to register to vote. Are
you registered?"

"No."

"But you pay taxes, don't you?"

"No, sir," the Negro replied, "I'm seventy-four, I'm on a
pension."

"But you did pay taxes when you were younger—you paid in
all that money, and the street out here doesn't have a curb and
doesn't have a sidewalk and the weeds down the corner are so tall
you can't see a car coming. . . ."

"Yes, sir. . . . That's sure right."

"Now, if people voted, wouldn't City Hall listen? Wouldn't things get better?"

"Yes, sir. . . . That's right."

"Well," the boy said, "we'd like to drive you down to the court-house to register. We can bring a car by your house tomorrow morning and bring you right back."

"I'm old," the man said, "I'm just too old to get into all that."

The boy pressed on, "But don't you see? You're *not* too old. You have a chance to leave a heritage of freedom. People will say, 'He stood up for freedom.' Don't you want to be free?"

"Yes, sir. That's right. . . . I just can't get my mind on all that. I just never voted, and I'm too old now." [15]

The student walked away, defeated for that day by barriers of caste and communication. Fortunately for Clarksdale, the per-sistence of Negro and white workers who returned again and again to the Riverton area began to overcome the traditional passivity. Soon, a cadre of several hundred Negro citizens had been formed. By early July, they established a branch of the Freedom Demo-cratic party and started a community development program. After COFO volunteers had worked in the area for only three weeks, the local Negroes felt sufficiently competent to start an organization of their own. At its inception, the Riverton precinct group elected leaders, formed investigatory committees, and gave expression to grievances which had never been spoken about before in public. At the inaugural meeting in a Baptist church, the Negroes at first hesitated to talk. After singing some freedom songs—and watching apprehensively as white cars circled the church—the Negroes fell into silence.

An old, toothless lady broke into the quiet atmosphere: "I'm not afraid to talk. I'm poor and old and I know what they can do to me. But the Lord will provide a piece of bread for me. Come on, talk! I've been in jail for seven days when I tried to vote—they know me, but I'm not afraid."

Amidst a chorus of amens, other people stood up. "Somebody

told me that there would be a bomb here," a muscled black man said, "but even if I die here, I die for something! We got to get up here and let that man in the White House know how we live—and he'll listen, too."

A torrent of complaints began. A maid described her work: "I get three dollars a day, sometimes only seventy-five cents. I do heavy work. I cook and I iron twenty pieces a day. I said to my white lady 'How am I to live? Your husband supports you, he's got money salted away, why can't you let my husband earn money?' She don't say nothing to me now."

Another woman spoke of voting: "How come they let only one out of ten of us vote in this town? We better start moving! I'll go down again tomorrow to register, if someone will come with me. What we need is unity."

A father talked of his children: "Those white people won't let my boys in the library. They won't let them go to a good school. Fifty children and one teacher—how can they learn anything that way?" He wanted new schools, but he wouldn't beg: "I'll teach my children at home. The whites can keep their schools, if they won't do no better. It's our taxes, our money—they aren't *giving* us schools." Just before sitting down, he added an afterthought which brought cheers, "They keep saying we have dumb children, but they don't say that they have a lot of lump-heads too."

The funeral parlor fans swished faster in everyone's hands, the hallelujahs grew more fervent as the silence of generations ended. The meeting that night marked a new era in Clarksdale—a beginning of an organized fight for the vote, for schools, streets and sewers, for a library and better salaries.

The whites struck back: On June 22, the police picked up four white freedom workers on vagrancy charges, releasing them after a three-hour interrogation; several days later, a truck with hidden license plates tried to run down two white volunteers; Negroes began to lose their jobs for registering to vote, and bomb threats flooded the COFO office. Local officials led the harassment. A white minister, driving an integrated car, reported that Sheriff Ben Collins asked him: "Are you married to them niggers? You ain't no minister, you're a SOB troublemaker . . . . . I'm gonna stay on your back until I get you." [16]

The same Sheriff arrested a Negro volunteer for failure to signal a turn. After a beating in jail, the volunteer said that the sheriff warned him: "You're a nigger and you're going to stay a nigger." [17]

Officials fined the boy for resisting arrest.

In the well-organized, well-led Negro section of Clarksdale, the white attack served only to stiffen Negro determination. By the end of June, an increasing number of pupils had joined the freedom school, attendance at rallies went up dramatically, and 1,200 Negroes had made out freedom registration forms. At the beginning of July, faced with an unprecedented number of applicants, the town closed its voter registration office.

As Aaron Henry said over national television: "Now the Negro acts, the white reacts. We are on our way, and we will make it."

With varying success—excellent in Clarksdale, meager in Moss Point—the movement spread throughout Mississippi. The older people sometimes held back, the middle-aged seemed fearful, but the young took the lead. "Someday, boy, you will take my place up here," said Aaron Henry, placing his hand on a teen-ager attending a Clarksdale rally. The boy's pride and the applause of his peers suggested that the compliment would soon be fact.

By the beginning of July, often due to the efforts of youth, tangible progress could be recorded in most of the state. In fifteen towns, freedom schools had been established with an initial enrollment of 2,000 children. Twenty thousand freedom registration forms had been gathered in the first weeks of the campaign. Thousands of eligible voters tried to register and several hundred were enfranchised. A thousand workers from the North found shelter and food within the Negro community. Twenty thousand Negroes committed themselves fully to the struggle as voter applicants, canvassing workers, teachers, messengers. A hundred thousand more people expressed their unity with the movement in small yet important gestures.

In the community which I first entered, for example, only one family in a block of twenty actively participated in civil rights work. The mother warmly welcomed us to her home, fed us, and gave us her own bed so that we might sleep. I thought that the family might be exceptional, but within a week it became apparent that everyone on the block gave what he could to the movement. One family living across the street sat up at night to warn of suspicious cars entering the area. Another man, a gas station mechanic, offered a free tank of gas. Every mother on the street brought over dinners of spare ribs and chicken, grits and peas— often when it meant that her own family had to go without meat. These gestures of support gave the movement perhaps its deepest significance, for they indicated that a new channel of white and Negro communication had been opened. It was this ordinary form of friendship between whites and blacks which most infuriated the segregationists.

The White Counterattack

The white forces maneuvered quietly and efficiently to meet the civil rights challenge. With what effect they could, the whites tried to mount a statewide legal attack: mayors ordered immigrants to register with the police; school boards, as in Carthage, called old laws into action to close freedom schools, and ordinances against "littering" often prevented the distribution of pamphlets.

When a legal approach seemed inadequate, the whites turned to subterfuge. On June 16, for example, Negroes attempted to attend Democratic party precinct conventions for the first time this century. State law, on paper, requires that all such meetings must be held publicly and that any registered Democratic voter is eligible to vote on resolutions and delegates. When Negro voters dared to make an appearance, however, they usually found that the conventions had mysteriously been cancelled.

In Meridian, Mississippi, two Negroes went to the Chalk School where a precinct convention had been announced. The Negroes waited outside, after being told that no precinct meeting would be held. After fifteen minutes, a police car drove up and a man who identified himself as a precinct vice-chairman announced that the meeting would be held inside the school. A few minutes later, he motioned to some whites standing near the door and told them to come over to a tree on the lawn. A Negro voter recorded in his affidavit, "We also started for the tree. As we approached, I heard the precinct vice-chairman say that he already had appointed a secretary and a slate of delegates. Then he said, 'That's all folks. See you in four years.' Mrs. Griggs and I felt that we couldn't do anything else, so we left." [18]

Throughout Mississippi, the same deception occurred. At times, Negro delegates outnumbered whites and succeeded in electing delegates to the county convention. In other places, the meetings never took place or, as in Batesville, precinct leaders quickly called up white voters to fill the gaps in their ranks. Twelve Negroes arrived on time in West Batesville, for example, but only three whites were present. The chairman stalled the meeting until sufficient telephone calls had been made to rally twelve more whites.

The semilegal tactics did not satisfy most white Mississipians, for the number of Negro schools, community centers, and voter applicants continued to grow. By the end of June a turn to violence came naturally to many frustrated whites.

"Mississippi's vocabulary of violence is varied and old," a white journalist, Frank Trippet, reported. A native of Mississippi, Trippet recorded the casual conversations that he heard when returning home from New York. "After covering no more than 28 miles of blacktop highway, I was listening to Mississipians justify the assassination of John F. Kennedy ('He had no business going down to Dallas and trying to stir up those people just to get votes')." [19] Without probing, Trippet overheard threats of massacre—"I mean there's gonna be some *killing* if these niggers start trying to get into cafés and things." [20] Even children had learned the bragging language of racial warfare. "A nigger get smart with me," a boy said, "I'll be on him like white on rice and turn that nigger every way but loose." [21]

This explosive atmosphere soon claimed its victims. A running record of incidents in June provides only a brief official record of the white counterattack:

June 16: The Mount Zion Baptist Church in Philadelphia burned to the ground. The church had been a center for Negro mass meetings and the site for a freedom school. Three Negroes in Philadelphia suffered beatings that night.

June 21: A Molotov cocktail exploded in the basement of the Sweet Rest Church in Brandon. During the evening, unknown attackers dynamited two houses in McComb. The families who occupied the homes had planned to give shelter to summer volunteers.

June 23: In Jackson, a white man fired into the home of the Reverend R. L. T. Smith. Smith, a venerable leader of the community and known as a "conservative" Negro, had once run for Congress. The white gunman escaped after a city truck had reportedly picked him up. In another area of Jackson, white men fired into Henderson's Café, hitting a Negro in the head.

June 25: The Church of the Holy Ghost in Clinton burned after a local white minister spoke to a Negro Bible class. This was the fifth firebombing in ten days by Mississippi arsonists.

June 26: Columbus police arrested seven voter registration workers for distributing literature without a permit. The court set bond at $400. In Jackson, a CORE field secretary, Ed Hollander, suffered a beating in the Hinds County jail, the third beating of a civil rights worker in the same jail.

June 28: During Mississippi's "Hospitality month," whites hit a civil rights worker from behind as he arrived in the Jackson railroad station.

June 29: Four whites in a pick-up truck shot into two cars owned by volunteers in Hattiesburg.

A hundred events of similar tenor occurred throughout Mississippi. The message was always the same: "We're going to get you SOB's" (as in a threatening call to the Jackson headquarters) or "You dirty niggers better know your place" (in the words of a Clarksdale police officer). The full meaning of these communications from the twisted white world became apparent on the night of June 21 in Philadelphia, Mississippi, when the three young freedom workers, Michael Schwerner, James Chaney, and Andrew Goodman were murdered. It was a deed which triggered a worldwide sensation and may yet prove to be the incident that, more than any other single event, forces Mississippi to face its future. The story of the multiple murder has been told and retold, but one illuminating incident requires recounting here. Before the bodies of the dead workers had been found, Michael Schwerner's wife expressed her anguish by trying twice to see Governor Johnson of Mississippi. Accompanied by the Reverend Edwin King and SNCC worker Robert Zellner, she went to the governor's mansion. There, Zellner said, he overheard Governor Johnson reply to an inquiry about the missing men in the following words: "Governor Wallace of Alabama and I are the only two people who know where they are and we're not telling." [22] Mrs. Schwerner said that Governor Johnson slammed and locked the door when he recognized her.

3

The First Inroads:
July, 1964

As the second wave of volunteers entered Mississippi, the bodies of Andrew Goodman, James Chaney, and Michael Schwerner had still not been found. A crew of sailors continued the search but in a formal, desultory fashion. Their investigation, as I observed it, had lost hope; the forests and swamps of Neshoba County seemed to obscure every sign of the missing trio. Their efforts were jeered by a gallery of white Mississippians, one of whom commented, "We throw two or three niggers in every year, to feed the fish."

While international attention focused on the tragic events in Philadelphia, quiet but significant progress was made on civil rights fronts in other parts of Mississippi. In McComb, the most primitive center of white resistance to integration began to break down. In Greenwood, Negroes gained their first entrance into the electoral process. And in Jackson, hotels, restaurants, and other public

facilities lowered the barriers of segregation. These advances—
quite different in nature and provoked by an unusual coalition of
forces—deserve attention for they marked the first time that the
walls of discrimination really came tumbling down.

McComb: A Thrust into the Southwest

"Anyone who goes in faces a high probability of death," Bob
Moses commented in early July about the dangerous situation in
McComb. He and the other COFO leaders had decided against
sending any volunteers into the Southwest area. Moses himself had
undergone a beating there in 1961, and five Negroes had been
killed in recent months. Yet Moses knew that the region could not
be left to its own resources. Racists would take the absence of civil
rights workers as a sign of timidity. Local Negroes would view it
as a complete and final defeat.

In his usual quiet fashion, Bob Moses told reporters: ". . . So
we will go in ourselves. Then nobody can accuse us of sending [the
students] in for the purpose of getting killed. Then the whole question will be whether the country will do for us and for the Negro
people what they have done for the volunteers." [1]

Down in McComb, a small town in the piney hill area near the
Louisiana border, Mayor Gordon Burke announced his disinterest
in protecting civil rights workers. "I don't care what the devil
happens to those people who come in here to stir up trouble," the
mayor said. "They come to cause trouble—well, what the devil do
you expect? If the monkey is on anyone's back, it is not on ours—
it's on the people's who come down here. I can't protect you,
buddy, if you come down to stir up trouble." [2]

COFO leaders chose only seven men, all seasoned workers, to
make the voyage to McComb. The decision to enter the Southwest
had to be made on their own. For a white man to go involved
particular danger. "You will stand out like I would in a Jackson

hotel," one Negro worker told Mendy Samstein, a white boy who debated the decision. "They'll cut you down three days after you get there."

Mendy and the Negro worker and I stayed at a home near McComb in early July, just at the time when the call for volunteers in the Southwest had been issued. We rested for the night in a farm surrounded by barbed wire and guarded with shotguns. The house had no running water, paint, or wallpaper, but its owner, a large farm woman with three children, had placed a five-course dinner on the table for us. After eating we sang some rather morbid variations on the freedom songs ("If you don't find me in the freedom movement, I'll be hanging from the old oak tree"). All of us tried to persuade Mendy that the trip to the Southwest might not be worth the risk. The slight intense man, a fledgling historian from Brandeis, listened quietly to our arguments.

"Kid, I know how you feel," an older Negro worker told him. "We all feel guilty about Mike and Chaney. Something has to be done to make up for what happened to them. We all feel that someone has to go to McComb; but look at it rationally. What can possibly be accomplished there except your own death?"

"That same argument was given to Bob Moses three years ago," Mendy said. "He had to come to Mississippi alone, but now look at the movement he created."

The Negro worker acknowledged Moses's courage but contended, "The situation is plenty different now. Bob had friends to help him. But the Southwest is just a murder trap. You would be leading the poor people there to a slaughter. Maybe you can afford to be killed, but what about the local people you bring into the movement? What about a father with five children?"

We all paused as the sound of a strange car came up the road. One of the men jumped to the window with his rifle. "Get out of the light," the older worker ordered him. We watched tensely until the car had reversed and pulled back down the road.

The Negro worker, turning to Mendy, reached the sharpest

point of his argument. "Look, I'm just scared to go there," he confessed. "I know myself. If I went, it's just because I wanted to be a hero. How about you? Maybe that's all you really want: 'Mendy Samstein Found Dead!' in headlines? Sure, it's easy enough for you to die, but you leave plenty of people behind. You can't just abandon those McComb people who would get involved."

But Mendy Samstein, driven undoubtedly by many motives, headed off toward McComb the next day.

Five nights later, Mendy lay sleeping in the white frame house which served as quarters for the civil rights workers in McComb. An unidentified assailant placed eight sticks of dynamite next to his bedroom.* The blast ripped a deep hole in the concrete driveway and shattered the outside of the house. Broken glass fell over him, but Mendy stayed alive.

The July 10 bombing in McComb was just one incident in a barrage of terrorism. Southwestern Mississippi had become known as a base for the Klan and organizations such as Americans for the Preservation of the White Race (APWR). The inhabitants of the area had long been bombarded with racist propaganda. In December of 1963, *The Freedom Fighter* warned southwestern whites about the NAACP:

> In reality it is the Nationally Associated American Communist Party. . . . The Communists are milking millions of dollars from the Negroes and some trashy white people to wage a war on you with. They have the help of the Kennedy Brats, the Roosevelts, the Martin Luther Kings, Roy Wilkins, the Ed Sullivans, the Huntleys and Brinkleys, the Drew Pearsons, the James Merediths, the Black Warren Court and a lot of foolish congressmen and senators.[3]

* Witnesses saw the bombing (and many of the subsequent outrages in McComb) but hesitated to report the identity of the attackers. A Negro porter in a local saloon overheard a white man telling openly how he had made a mistake in placing the dynamite. "Next week, I'll do it better," he said. Observing the Negro watching him, the white man warned that he would blow up the Negro's house if he reported the conversation to the FBI.

With the usual genuflection to the myth that a Communist plot inspired the Negro revolt, another tract published in 1964 told its readers in McComb:

> The poor old American negro that you see driving these new Cadillacs up and down the road, while you are driving your behind off trying to pay doctor bills, grocery bills, notes on a home for your wife and children . . . you can bet if you check real hard, he had one or more negro women on Welfare that are drawing checks for a half dozen illegitimate negro kids. . . . And we'll bet that the mother of those kids is out begging some White for something.[4]

Indignantly, the pamphlet noted that "The Federal Government says that these people are to be placed in a position of society in life above you and me!" Another 1964 pamphlet, handed from door to door in the Southwest, brought out the inevitable argument that equality of opportunity would lead to "race-mixing":

> You can never have social and political equality with the Negro without asking him to your home sooner or later. If you seat him at your table he takes the right to ask your daughter's hand in marriage. The man or woman of Negro ancestry, though a century removed, will suddenly breed back to a pure Negro child. Kinky-headed, flat-nosed, thick lipped, black skinned. ONE DROP of Negro blood in your family could push it backward three thousand years in history.* [5]

In July, a typical representative of these organizations addressed a congregation in the Southwest. C. O. Stegall, a Baptist minister, made a speech to members of the Americans for the Preservation of the White Race. "Don't do no violence," he told them. "If they come into your store, close your doors and go home, God bless your soul . . . if the nigger can allow ketchup and raw eggs to be

---

* Since some supposedly educated people in the North believe this biological rubbish, it may deserve some comment. According to the best genetic estimates, about one-fifth of all "white" Southerners have Negro ancestors. Every American Negro has at least one white ancestor. The groups have been so intermixed already that it is impossible to talk of biologically distinct white or Negro "races" in the South.

rubbed into his head, why can't we do the same? The day that we kill three or four, they'd be martial law in Mississippi. My friends, we have to make up our minds that we're not going to run off at the head." [6]

The APWR claimed repeatedly that it adhered to nonviolent means. Yet the FBI had had to investigate forty acts of violence against Negroes in the Southwest during the preceding year. And during just one night in southern Mississippi and Louisiana, some unknown group burned three hundred crosses. Not a single person would admit to having witnessed this mass operation.

Everyone knew that the racist organizations used economic boycotts to keep business in line. Earlier in the year, Kenneth Tolliver, a staff writer for *The Delta Democrat-Times,* drew a parallel between Nazi methods and those of new segregationist organizations. Tolliver reported how local businessmen in the Southwest received threatening telephone calls ordering them to fire Negroes who had been "offensive." One merchant in Liberty refused a demand to fire a trusted Negro employee. "Within twenty-four hours," Tolliver reported, "a strangling boycott had been set up against his business. The society (APWR) stationed workers near his front door who copied the names of anyone who went into the business . . . as the weeks went by and the merchant found himself not only on the brink of economic disaster but also effectively locked out of the town social life, he gave in and fired the Negro." [7]

A minister in Liberty had to find a new pulpit after he protested a hate-mongering meeting. A doctor received a call which mentioned the ease with which his children could be hurt on the way to school. Negroes who joined the NAACP lost their homes. "All we have to do," a speaker told an APWR audience, "is to make white people raise rents until the Negro is forced to move away. Of course we will do it gradually so that their loss will not affect our economy." [8]

After reporting the growth of these secret societies in the Southwest—there "no one sees anything, says anything or does anything"—Kenneth Tolliver himself was threatened. One night in June, while staying at the home of his Pulitzer Prize-winning editor, Hodding Carter, he answered the phone and heard, "We have read your articles on the Americans for the Preservation of the White Race, and we understand you plan to do a series. We want you to know that we know how to take care of you if you do." Forty-five minutes later, he received another call. "We forgot to tell you," a voice said, "we've killed other people . . . you wouldn't be the first." [9]

Violence came easily to racists in the Southwest. During the month of July alone, they bombed not only the COFO headquarters in McComb, but also five churches which had been used for civil rights meetings. Although a brave white witness indentified two cars which carried men to the burning of several churches in Kingston on July 13, the police found themselves incapable of tracing the arsonists.

The civil rights workers who entered this area obviously faced a formidable challenge. A few of them, like the Reverend Don McCord, attempted to make contact with whites in McComb and the surrounding communities. McCord found most of the white ministers to be unresponsive to pleas for racial tolerance. "I've never had no trouble with niggers," a typical Baptist minister said, "but I won't allow them in my church."

Some whites in McComb tried to moderate the passions of their fellow citizens. A local insurance man, for example, agreed to talk with civil rights workers in early July. The conversations resulted in an agreement by the businessman to issue an appeal to his fellow townsmen for tolerance. Other whites, however, soon learned of the meeting between the insurance salesman and the civil rights workers. They immediately set up a blockade of his business. By the end of the month, the businessman had to close his office and send his wife, who suffered from nervous exhaustion, to an adjoining town. He published a public confession of his "errors" in the town newspaper.

Some workers, like Dennis Sweeney and Mendy Samstein, went into the Negro community. There they found a great longing for freedom, but also paralyzing fear. When a few Negroes volunteered their homes for meetings, they were swamped with threats from whites. When Negro ministers used their churches for civil rights meetings, the buildings were bombed. It appeared, at the middle of July, that the whites' terrorism had succeeded in subduing the town's Negro population.

On July 16, however, the tide began to turn when 108 children first attended the McComb freedom school. The school had been announced with some hesitation, since COFO workers feared that parents might be too frightened to send their children.

Nonetheless, the children demanded the school and responded enthusiastically to the teachers. During the first days, classes met on a country lawn, since no housing could be found. By the end of July, a courageous minister had offered his church, St. Paul's Methodist, to shelter the school.

The children published a weekly newspaper with a cover which showed a kneeling Negro asking, "Am I not a man and a brother?" One of the writers, Joyce Brown, composed a poem designed to shake the older people of McComb from their fear. In part, she said:

> I asked for your churches, and you
>   turned me down
> But I'll do my work if I have to do it
>   on the ground,
> You will not speak for fear of being heard
> So crawl in your shell and say, "Do not disturb."
> You think because you've turned me away
> You've protected yourself for another day.

Joyce Brown reminded the adult Negroes that "tomorrow surely must come" and that the enemy would still be there.

Surprisingly, the poem, and perhaps their children's bravery, brought an unexpectedly strong response from McComb Negroes.

All the local Negro businessmen met together in late July. Several wept when they heard the poem read. They responded to its request "to stand tall and be a man" by pledging their houses, money, and influence to civil rights work. Other adults took the dangerous step of trying to register to vote, and a thousand people became "freedom registered" voters. For the first time in memory, Negroes held public rallies in the fields surrounding the town. As in many parts of the state, the children led the way by shaming their parents into acts of bravery.

The whites continued to apply pressure. The local Klan leader, an oil dealer with a third-grade education, circled COFO headquarters each night in his Cadillac. He prominently displayed a powerful rifle. Unknown whites still threw bombs at Negro churches and homes. And a night guard had to be mounted around the houses where civil rights workers slept.

Nonetheless, a spirit of resistance had come into the McComb Negro community. "The Freedom Train is coming, coming, coming . . . ," little girls sang as they played on the grass in front of the bombscarred COFO building, "The Freedom Train is coming, and we'll all get aboard." McComb's whites had never heard that song before.

Greenwood: A Freedom Day

I must admit that my hand shook as I took notes on the potential voters who filed toward the Greenwood registrar's office on July 16. Police in helmets and cowboy hats glowered at us as Negroes entered the forbidden sanctum to place their names on the voting roll. Outside, a Greenwood police captain snapped pictures of each person in the line. The Negroes knew that the photographs would be used to indentify them and that they might well lose their homes or jobs. Yet more than a hundred of them still came forward in silent pace. That day, more Negroes registered to vote in

Greenwood than ever before.

Greenwood's "Freedom Day" came only after a laborious build-up. The Negroes in Greenwood lived in deplorable conditions which did little to inspire direct, constructive action on their part: 87 per cent of them earned less than $3,000 a year; of the county 131 hospital beds, only 37 could be used by Negroes; while some 14,000 Negroes were eligible to vote, just 258 people had been allowed to pass the test imposed by the Greenwood registrar. The Pearl River divides the town and, as one Negro told me, "Plenty of people, including Mack Parker, have floated down it." Greenwood —a scrubby island in a sea of cotton, bigotry, and violence—had earned a cruel reputation. If a "nigger" tried to vote in Greenwood, this was the height of insolence.

In the weeks preceding Freedom Day, however, a series of religiously toned meetings had inspired Greenwood Negroes. Lawyers informed them of their constitutional rights: "If a policeman stops you, you can always ask what the charge is—but around here, it's probably not wise." SNCC leaders answered the sometimes pathetic questions posed by the audiences. "My mother is blind," one man said, "and those voting men, they won't read her the application. They keep turning her away. Don't she have a right to hear the questions?" However discouraging the answers, the people always ended the meetings with clapping choruses of "I've Got the Light of Freedom."

The SNCC organization, headed by James Forman, moved its national headquarters to Greenwood. Convinced that the town was ready for a "massive confrontation," the civil rights workers made provisions for a car pool, a messenger service, and legal aid for potential voters. For years the town had been the focus of agitation. Now the great majority of Negroes was ready to press for its rights. Moreover, whites in the city could no longer use terrorism with quite the same abandon as in the past, since FBI agents and journalists from across the nation watched events in Greenwood with new care.

Richard Frey, director of the local Freedom House, set July 16 as the target date for testing voter discrimination in Greenwood. The day dawned bright and hot. Knots of Negroes gathered in front of churches, waiting patiently for cars to take them to city hall. The short drive there was a crucial voyage for many of them, a time when they had to display all the courage they possessed. As I drove one old woman, trying to vote for the first time, she commented, "I never did this before, because I know how they treat people. But last night I heard such good singing and talk and prayer at the church, I felt I couldn't let them down. So I prayed all night and God, he listened to me. He told me to come." When we pulled in front of the brick Victorian mansion which served as a city hall, we could see that many Negroes had already lined up. About a hundred sheriff's deputies, regular and auxiliary police surrounded them. Police vans stood poised around the corner.

The police ordered Negroes to keep a single line, stay off the grass, and not display any signs. By 9 A.M. scores of young Negroes, below voting age, had come to watch their elders. COFO workers kept orderly lines as, one by one, the Negroes approached the entrance. As slowly as they could, police allowed the Negroes to enter. Many were turned down. An old man, Lucius Ledbetter, reported that the registrar would not take his name and address. Sarah Brock failed the test because she did not know her precinct number. The majority of applicants, however, were allowed to take the test for the first time in Greenwood memory.

Outside the courthouse, restless younger people held up signs asking for the vote. They began singing "Before I'll be a slave, I'll by lying in my grave." Chief of police Curtis Larry barked over a megaphone: "There will be no picketing!" The singing did not stop since the Negroes wished to challenge the consitutionality of the state's antipicketing rules. The police charged the line grabbing young and old people at random. By 10:15, police had loaded forty demonstrators into a wire-meshed prison van. More Negroes, many of them children, picked up the signs dropped by the prisoners.

The police charged again. This time, they used billies and electric prods designed for cattle. A pregnant woman screamed at the police when officers choked her under the neck with a club. They dragged her to a waiting van. Waves of police kept coming until 115 people had been arrested. As busloads of Negroes went off to jail, other people chanted "Free-dom, Free-dom, Free-dom!"

The most elderly people remained in line, waiting stoically upon the registrar's pleasure. The heat grew more intense as the afternoon continued. Since people had to stand for five or six hours (the police refused to allow any sitting), the strain was great. "Are you holding up all right," I asked one cheerful old lady as I walked up and down the line. "Sure," she replied, "I've picked cotton all my life on these legs. They can hold me up now to vote."

At the jail, Judge O. L. Kimbrough presided. Sallow and plump, the judge had become renowned for his treatment of previous civil rights cases. His lunch had been interrupted and he was in no mood to deal lightly with the cases before him. When a lawyer and I went to jail to inquire about the picketers, Judge Kimbrough snapped at the lawyer, "Why are you here? Are you looking for a job? Can't you get enough work in your own state?" The judge wanted to schedule the case for immediate trial. When the lawyer pointed out the difficulty of consulting 115 clients in fifteen minutes, the judge relented and allowed the lawyer to consult with a few prisoners.

Several days later, the judge convicted all demonstrators over fifteen years of age. Only a few of the defendants had been given the right to counsel. While those without bail had to wait in jail, their cases were appealed on grounds that restrictions on peaceful picketing constituted an obvious infringement of freedom of speech.

As was their habit, city officials charged that Communists lurked behind the Freedom Day. Citing such impeccable sources as Senator Eastland, the mayor and city officials noted the large telephone bill paid by the SNCC office and the $12,000 in bail posted for demonstrators. Using their own brand of reasoning, the city officials seemed to feel that this evidence was sufficient proof of outside Communist influences.

While the jail sentences caused sorrow in Greenwood, the Negro community could still rejoice. Many Negroes (and more were to come) had jumped the hurdles to voting. The whites had tried every means to discourage registration, but when faced with a unified Negro group, a large majority of the population, the whites had grudgingly given way. Economic sanctions had played their part. Some white merchants who had been among the more brutal of the auxiliary police found their businesses sharply declining after July 16. As one Negro, a father who saw two of his children taken to jail, later told me, "We taught them here that they can't treat us like animals any more."

Ethics and Economics in Jackson

After a historic legal battle, President Lyndon Johnson signed the Civil Rights Bill into law on July 2, 1964. "The purpose of the law is simple," he said. "It does not restrict the freedom of any American so long as he respects the right of others. It does not give special treatment to any citizen. . . . It does say that those who are equal before God shall now also be equal in the polling booths, in the classrooms, in the factories, and in hotels and restaurants and movie theaters, and other places that provide service to the public."

The new law provoked anguished cries in Mississippi. The governor and the White Citizens' Councils called upon the people to disobey the law, newspapers trumpeted the perfidy of the "communist-socialist-liberal clique" in Washington, and Confederate flags flew at half-mast. The Citizens' Councils established a "dial-the-truth" service where people could telephone day or night to hear a transcript of advice on how to disobey the law. Racist whites could well feel grieved, for the law tore away most of the last legal excuses for segregation. The provisions which most directly affected the state and excited the deepest wrath were those by which:

—The Attorney General of the United States received new powers to speed up court hearings of civil rights cases, particularly when the issue at stake involved a systematic refusal to allow Negroes to vote. With new authority to initiate federal suits, the government could avoid the legal delays which had characterized Mississippi judicial process. (Suits on voting discrimination, for example, had been submitted in 1961, but were not heard until 1964.) As a consequence, the five counties in Mississippi where over 50 per cent of the population was Negro, but not a single Negro had been enfranchised, faced the imminent prospect of federal prosecution.

—Discrimination on the basis of race, color, religion, or national origin was prohibited in all public accommodations. In the past, Negroes sometimes had to travel 175 miles across the South before finding food or lodging. Title II of the new law eased this situation by giving all men a legal right to public shelter and food.

—The federal government was empowered to cut off money from projects in which ethnic discrimination is found. In Mississippi, a state receiving millions of dollars from the national pocketbook, this provision could have profound impact.

—A new bureau, the Equal Employment Opportunity Commission, was created to oversee the policies and practices of businesses and unions.

—Several sections, aimed directly at Mississippi, provided that civil rights cases could be removed from the jurisdiction of state courts and that a federal survey of voting discrimination should be conducted. Such a study could be used under the Fourteenth Amendment to reduce the congressional representation of those states that excluded the Negro from politics.

—The Attorney General and the Commissioner of Education received power to institute punitive legal proceedings and cut off federal aid from school districts which continued to disobey the Supreme Court decision of 1954.

As the bill became the law of the land, white spokesmen in Mississippi predicted that it could not be implemented. For their part, extremist whites forthrightly announced their lawlessness. Governor Johnson said he anticipated "some real trouble." A journalist asked the governor whether Mississippians should try to obey the law. "No," answered the governor, "I don't think they should." At a speech in Gulfport, the governor added, "They can pass all the laws they want, but they can't make us like it or take it." Moderate whites, particularly businessmen who feared for the state's economic future, expected mob violence. On the night of July 1, members of Jackson's economic elite kept in close telephone contact with Washington officials, consulting about the possible use of federal marshals to curtail mob reactions.

Within the Negro community, a split developed about the proper strategy to follow. Some leaders, like Charles Evers of the NAACP, promised that extensive testing of the law's strength would soon come. Evers and a delegation from the national board of the NAACP planned to launch a direct-action program throughout the state. COFO leaders, on the other hand, wanted to delay any attempts to desegregate public facilities. They reasoned that white public opinion had become too inflamed to try still another challenge to what they regarded as a minor aspect of the segregated system. Subsequent events proved that COFO leaders underestimated both the Negro's desire to use public facilities and the white businessman's willingness to comply with the law.

Although there were pockets of resistance, the initial response to the law was strongly, surprisingly positive. Negroes played golf on Jackson's municipal course, ate at a Vicksburg lunch counter, and drank cokes in a Hattiesburg dime store. A Negro basketball star, together with some Catholic priests, ate in Jackson's Sun-N-

Sand luxury motel. The clerk said simply, "Sign in, please." News-men and detectives watched while guests paid little attention.

Members of the NAACP executive board toured the state, test-ing the new law. Escorted by grim, red-faced highway patrolmen and local police during most of its trip, the group integrated hotels and restaurants in Jackson, Meridian, Laurel, and Biloxi. By the end of the tour, it appeared that most hotel managers had accepted the new development with grace. At the Markham Hotel near Gulfport, the smiling desk clerk even uttered the South's tradi-tional, "Y'all come back again now. . . ." The tensest moment of the trip came when the group visited Philadelphia. They were stopped by Neshoba County prosecutor Raiford Jones and an angry crowd armed with bottles and guns. When Jones called the men "boy" and "nigger," attorney Robert Carter said, "Mr. Jones, you don't know me well enough to call me by my first name." Jones replied, "We'll call you anything we want down here . . . as far as we're concerned, you don't have any kind of rights down here." Except for some occasions of rudeness, however, the trip succeeded in its basic aim of demonstrating Negro access to public facilities.

A mood of mild euphoria went through the Negro community as unorganized groups of people spontaneously entered local hotels and restaurants. In Jackson, word spread immediately after every success. ("Did you hear?" one neighbor would ask another, "the Heidelberg just fed some people.") In Hattiesburg, the day after the law was passed, apprehensive but still happy teen-agers went from store to store filling themselves with soda-pop.

The Negroes only laughed at the white resisters. In Jackson, the Robert E. Lee hotel put up a sign: "Closed in Despair. Civil Rights Bill Unconstitutional!" While the hotel owner talked of his southern patriotism, local gossip of Negroes soon told of the hotel's near-bankrupt condition which had actually forced its clos-ing. And Primos's restaurants in Jackson drew laughs as their owner, head of the White Citizens' Council doubled the armed police guard around the doors. The Jackson Negro newspaper *Free Press* summed up the Negro response when it headlined, "Jackson Astounds the Nation." The city had finally proved its willingness to maintain law and order.

Inevitably, there were some trouble spots in other parts of the state. In Laurel, on July 4, several Negroes sought service at a drive-in café from a window reserved for whites. The owner threatened then with a shotgun and other whites attacked with knives. In the resulting fight, two Negroes and two whites received knife wounds. In Clarksdale, Negroes attempted to integrate restaurants, theaters, and other public facilities without success. City officials closed the local swimming pools. At a barber shop in Clarksdale, the owner said he would kill Negroes and brandished a revolver at them. The Clarksdale justice of the peace refused to hear a complaint about the barber, and later the chief of police arrested the lawyer who had tried to have the law enforced.

Despite these incidents, the pattern in the state was on the whole one of quiet compliance. Some white leaders, such as the head of the Mississippi Catholic church, issued pleas for peace and order. On July 3, Bishop Richard Gerow, a native of Mobile and a bishop for forty years, urged his parishioners to "accept the action of Congress as loyal Americans and . . . give the world an example of true patriotism in a democracy."

Much of the credit for the pattern of peaceful evolution in the state should go to enlightened white businessmen, a group of moderates that some civil rights workers had too easily discounted. Typifying the attitude of the economic elite, the Jackson Chamber of Commerce passed a resolution calling for compliance with the civil rights law.* This action, together with a similar request from the mayor of Jackson, guided the response of many of the state's

* The Mississippi House of Representatives immediately met in extraordinary session to censure the Chamber of Commerce. "This deplorable act of calling for slavish obedience," the House declared, "is a contravention of everything the State of Mississippi has fought for and stands for . . . it constitutes aid and comfort to the integrationist, communist and socialist minorities of the nation." [10]

businessmen.

The resolution represented the first time that moderate white leaders in the community *effectively* acted to calm a potentially violent situation. One member of the Chamber's board of directors explained to me why Jackson's economic elite had taken action.

This man (who asked to remain anonymous for fear of retaliation) regarded himself as a political conservative. Mississippi-born and the owner of a large business, the executive had long claimed a place among the ruling figures in the state. In the days preceding the passage of the Civil Rights Act, he had watched the pressure for compliance build up. "Various small businessmen came to the Chamber for guidance," he recalled. "At least thirty businessmen went to the major banks to see if they could get loans to fight the civil rights law. Luckily, the banks turned them down."

On the night of July 1, the businessman and some clergymen telephoned John Doar at the Justice Department in Washington. "The national government told us that a forthright announcement from the Chamber would go far in keeping down passions. If Jackson could comply, it would establish the pattern for the state." On July 2, the Chamber's board of directors met in secrecy with Mayor Thompson and the presidents of two local banks. "It was clear to all of us that the law had to be obeyed. The purpose of our resolution was to give the mayor and the governor some room to maneuver. They could not afford the political cost of standing up for compliance all by themselves." The next night, the Chamber approved the resolution with only four dissenting votes. "We knew we would be attacked," my informant said, "but a little public flurry couldn't hurt us as individual businessmen. The Citizens' Council jumped at our necks, of course, but these days the Council is made up only of economic parvenus. The Legislature censured us but that was just a grandstand play. Eighty-two members signed the condemnation without reading it when it was just a blank piece of paper."

Most of the Chamber's members voted for compliance out of

purely economic motives. "Two-thirds would probably have liked to disobey the law," the businessman said, "but they couldn't afford to carry on a hopeless legal battle."

The businessman typified the attitude of Mississippi's upper class. He deplored the rowdiness of racists, disbelieved the usual propaganda about white superiority, and feared the economic consequences of lawlessness. "Most of the businessmen stand for 'law and order.' After all, we demanded compliance with the ridiculous laws which we passed against the Negro. It would be rather silly now to reverse ourselves when we don't like new laws."

While the economic elite could be counted upon to maintain civic stability, it acted only in response to outside pressure. All of its members with whom I talked were too afraid to do anything on their own to initiate racial progress. The businessman's experience illustrated the elite's behavior and its fears. "Five years ago," he remembered, "I protested when my church wanted to censor some Sunday school literature which supposedly advocated integration. Really, they wanted to eliminate the Book of Ruth from the Bible. After I said that was silly, I began to get abusive phone calls at my house calling me a 'nigger-lover.' And my dealers warned me to keep my mouth shut. After that, I learned to be more careful of what I said."

This slight exposure to racist harassment was sufficient to keep the businessman publicly in line. "I would like to have Negroes in my home, and I'd like to see the schools opened to them, but I can't say it or I'd lose my business," he remarked rather apologetically.

Nonetheless, in standing up for a respectable cause such as obeying the law, this man and his fellows in the economic elite could act in a helpful, decisive way. They made useful allies in the fight for civil rights, but they have never been found in the vanguard. Progress has to be initiated by the Negroes themselves. And even the most forceful Negro action will have little effect unless the federal government reinforces it.

The Federal Presence

During July, the civil rights movement gained steady momentum. The opening of McComb's freedom school, the gain of several hundred voters in Greenwood, the fact that Negroes could eat in Jackson restaurants—these might seem like insignificant advances. Yet each in its own way meant a great deal to Mississippi Negroes.

White racists continued to burn churches, attack volunteers, and threaten local Negroes. Left to their own devices, the bigots might well have massacred their opponents, but their resistance seemed to lessen as Negro audacity grew.

The white restraint did not occur spontaneously. What made the difference was that Mississippi, for the first time since its total defeat at Vicksburg, learned of the full power of a determined national government. In a variety of ways, much more pervasively than during the Oxford crisis, Mississippians felt the federal presence.

In several symbolic ways, the nation made its influence apparent. Northern congressmen toured the state in early July and reported the pattern of discrimination. On July 11, J. Edgar Hoover visited Jackson and opened a new office of the FBI. He announced that the agency's force in the area had been increased by fifty officers. An unsmiling Governor Johnson met Hoover. Mayor Thompson, outwardly a segregationist, shook Hoover's hand and said, "I'm mighty glad you're here." By this point, FBI agents in the state exceeded 150 men. For the first time in recent Mississippi history, federal agents arrested some white men for threatening civil rights workers and Negroes.

The U.S. Commission on Civil Rights held open meetings at Jackson at the end of the month. Martin Luther King went to several cities to address rallies for the Negro-based Freedom

Democratic party. Civil rights groups, to the surprise of their opponents, secured "John Doe" warrants and initiated federal suits against white terrorists. And court cases requiring school integration approached their culmination.

Above all, national concern about the safety of civil rights workers kept the state in the forefront of American attention. Around the Bogue Chitto swamp, the search for the missing civil rights workers continued as teams of FBI agents and sailors from the Naval Air Station at Meridian trudged the back hills around the area. While local newspapers still tried to dismiss the kidnapping as a hoax, the suspicion deepened that Mississippi whites had killed the workers.

Due to this national support—and of course to the sustained effort of local Negroes—the minimum goals of the COFO project had already been fulfilled by the end of July. Forty thousand Negroes had joined the Freedom Democratic party. Thirty freedom schools in nineteen communities (far in excess of those planned in June) had opened their doors. The Civil Rights Bill had been implemented at least partially in many sections of the state.*

All these advances gave comfort to Mississippi Negroes and to the northern "invaders." Yet no one could rest easily. August in Mississippi is known as a time when the smoldering heat can cause an almost insanely violent attitude. It is during this period that forest fires, many of them deliberately set aflame, flare up at their greatest intensity. And in the old days, August was the month when lynchings reached their peak. The following days were also scheduled as the first time that school integration would be tried on a large scale in Mississippi. The next month, most civil rights leaders believed, would be decisive.

---

* Contrary to liberal scoffers, the Civil Rights Bill did in fact give some aid to even the poorest of Mississippi Negroes. Admittedly, only a handful of middle-class Negroes could go into the restaurants usually reserved for whites, but many Negroes from all classes flocked to the cafés, drive-ins, and dime-store counters opened by the new law.

4

A Bitter Taste of Victory:
August, 1964

AT the beginning of August, state and local police abandoned
the search for the three missing civil rights workers. Mississippi's
leaders assured their people that the Philadelphia incident had
been a hoax, one more devilish trick played by the agitators. Senator Eastland hinted that the three young men had run away voluntarily and that Communists had plotted their disappearance. "They
could be in Cuba," Governor Johnson said airily.

On August 4, however, Mississippi's fantasy ended.

Six weeks after the search began, FBI men, acting on the information of a "reliable source," secured a warrant to search a farm
three miles southwest of Philadelphia. The owner, a burly trucker
named Olen Burrage, told the agents "to look all they wanted" on
his Old Jolly farm. In 101-degree heat, FBI agents spread out over
the farm. A bulldozer pulled off Highway 21, rammed a path
through scrubby pine trees, and aimed its blade at a freshly built
dam. An excavator chewed a hole into the base of the 20-foot high

wall of red clay, and there, as the informant had told them, the FBI men found the decomposed bodies of James Chaney, Andrew Goodman, and Michael Schwerner.

Pathologists recorded that all three men had been killed by 38-caliber revolver slugs. Initial reports from the University of Mississippi Medical Center said that none of them had suffered a beating. Later, another autopsy was requested by Chaney's mother. It showed that James Chaney, the Negro, had been savagely beaten. His skull had been fractured in several places, pieces of broken bone had entered his brain, and he had multiple fractures in other places, including a smashed shoulder and arm. Governor Paul Johnson, in almost his only public statement after the discovery, treated the autopsy in cryptic fashion: "Informed people know that extremist Negro groups will issue any statement they feel will influence the public mind in the attempt to raise money for their deceptive projects." [1]

Other reactions of Mississippi whites ranged from mild regret to simple irritation. Congressman Arthur Winstead expressed an incredible "It's too bad, but . . ." attitude, typical of Mississippi morality. After commenting that the discovery of the bodies had "ended anxiety," he added, "However, when people leave any section of the county and go into another section looking for trouble, they can usually find it." [2]

In Philadelphia itself, some residents expressed regret at the murders. Olen Burrage, whose farm hid the bodies, talked affably with newsmen, "I tell you," he said, "I just don't know of anyone who would have killed them and put them on my property." [3] Burrage had hired a workman, Herman Tucker, to build the dam as a means of creating a pond for his cows. Tucker had worked since May on the dam. "He just told me to build it and I built it," Tucker said. His comment on the dead men: "I don't know nothing about it, don't care nothing about it, and don't want to discuss it." [4] Newsmen reported that Philadelphia residents were more concerned with the identity of the informer (who had supposedly received $30,000) than with the murderers. "There's something un-American about it," one Philadelphia man said about the informer.[5]

President Lyndon Johnson promised a thorough follow-up investigation, and FBI agents let slip the news that they expected to arrest suspects very soon. Local residents gossiped freely about the murderers. One story, spread by an FBI agent, blamed four police officers. Another rumor named two policemen, a preacher, a bootlegger, a used-car dealer, and a TV repairman. Nonetheless, no arrests were made and, by the middle of August, Philadelphia Sheriff Laurence Rainey brazenly dismissed FBI agents who had been questioning him.* He refused his cooperation with the comment, that if they returned, they had better come with subpoenas. The agents did return with warrants.

On October 3, the FBI arrested Sheriff Rainey, Deputy Price, and two other men on charges of "violating the rights of Negro citizens." Unfortunately, however, only state authorities can indict the murderers of the civil rights workers. Local officials, responding to fears expressed by the white population, reassured people that those suspected of murder would appear before a Mississippi rather than a Federal court for their crime. The whites relaxed again in the conviction that the most recent killers—like the murderers of Till, Parker, Lee, Allen, Evers, and the hundreds of others who have died because of race violence—would receive the kindest attention from Mississippi's elastic system of justice.

The relatives of the murdered men received the news of the killings with dignity and restraint. Mrs. Rita Schwerner told newsmen: "To me, three good men were killed—three good men who could have done a great deal for their country." When newsmen asked her what good might come of her husband's death, she responded: "That, I imagine, is up to the people of the United States." In New York, Andrew Goodman's parents also expressed

* In a stance typical of the quality of Mississippi justice, the Mississippi State Bar Association had previously informed Mississippians that they had no obligation to cooperate in the enforcement of civil rights laws.

a hope that their son's death had not been totally in vain. "Our grief, though personal, belongs to the nation," Mr. Robert Goodman said in a faltering voice. "This tragedy is not private. . . . For ourselves, we wish to express our pride in our son's commitment and that of his companions now alive, now in Mississippi. . . ." [6]

The murdered men's comrades in Mississippi vowed to go on. At a memorial service in Meridian for James Chaney, CORE's Dave Dennis, a Negro leader, said that COFO would continue its "block-by-block, county-by-county" fight to register voters—"And if they're not ready for me, too bad, baby, 'cause I'm coming anyway. . . . Don't just look at me and go home and say that was a nice memorial service. If you go home tonight and take it, goddam your soul!" [7]

The fight did proceed and, as events unfolded, it went on with increasing success. The advances of August—in education, in political organization, in repulsing further white attacks—gave the dead men the noble epitaph which they so clearly deserved.

The School Barriers Fall

Integrationists and white moderates in the state looked to August, 1964, as *the* test period of school integration. Moving a single Negro into the University of Mississippi had involved thousands of federal troops and two deaths. Now, Federal courts had enjoined three entire counties to end forthwith their attempts to maintain segregation. For the first time since 1954, Negro children would attempt to enter some of the primary schools of Mississippi.

As the bastion of school segregation, the state in August, 1964, hardly seemed ready to allow equality of opportunity in education. The history of past attempts to enforce the Supreme Court decision was a sorry record of repeated failures and white obduracy.

Following the 1954 Supreme Court decision, statements of

fanatic opposition had appeared in every influential journal in the state. In Jackson, the *Daily News* editorialist wrote: "Human blood may stain Southern soil in many places [but] . . . Mississippi cannot and will not try to abide by such a decision." [8] Mississippi Supreme Court Judge Tom P. Brady gave segregationists their bible in his *Black Monday*. According to Brady (who continued his ten-year-long leadership of the battle against integration), slavery had helped the Negro. "The American Negro was divorced from Africa and saved from savagery," Brady wrote, ". . . a moral standard of values was presented to him, a standard he could never have created for himself and which he does not now appreciate." [9] The Communists, through the NAACP, the CIO, and President Roosevelt, had conceived a complex plot. In Brady's view, "The Negro proposes to breed up his inferior intellect and whiten his skin, and 'blow out the light' in the white man's brain and muddy his skin." [10] Such preachings had originally spawned the White Citizens' Councils, with their effective instruments of economic terror as well as a series of rear-guard legal actions.

With the creation in early 1956 of the State Sovereignty Commission, the ruling powers in Mississippi had more or less assured the temporary silence of Mississippi Negroes. The commission drew its support from tax funds and was authorized to "do and perform any and all acts and things deemed necessary and proper to protect the sovereignty of the state of Mississippi." From its inception the commission employed secret investigators and informers charged with the task of maintaining segregation. For a decade, despite intermittent lawsuits, the commission had succeeded in fulfilling its mission of suppressing liberty. The state's lawyers succeeded in evading the Supreme Court decision, with all deliberate slowness, until July of 1964.

On July 8 of that year, the Federal courts ordered school desegregation in three Mississippi towns: Jackson (the state's capital), Biloxi (a sea-coast resort receiving a high proportion of federal aid), and Carthage (the primitive hill town near Philadelphia). Ironically, the lawsuit which precipitated segregation's downfall had been lodged on behalf of Kenyatta Evers, son of the slain NAACP leader. The resulting court order forced the Jackson school district to allow Evers to enroll in white public schools. U.S. District Judge Sidney Mize told the school boards that they had to integrate their first grades immediately, and additional grades successively for the next twelve years. Judge Mize, known for his belief in Negro inferiority, acted with reluctance. In his decision, the judge cited evidence purporting to show that Negroes had smaller brains and less intelligence.*

He claimed that "the facts in this case point up a most serious [prospect], and indeed cry out for a reappraisal and complete reconsideration of the findings and conclusions" reached by the Supreme Court. Nonetheless, despite his beliefs, Judge Mize could not once again ignore the weight of legal decisions holding segregation unconstitutional.

Legal battles flurried in July and August: the school boards tried to delay the order's execution and the NAACP, on its part, argued that the proposed "grade-a-year" plan did not fulfill completely the Supreme Court's intention. Both sides, however, cor-

---

* Because Judge Mize's views represent the opinions not only of the majority of Mississippi whites but also of many formally educated Americans, they deserve some comment. The average American Negro does indeed have a somewhat smaller brain than the average American white. But brain size has no proven relation to intelligence. Indeed, the largest brain on record was possessed by an idiot and Einstein had a remarkably small brain.[11]

The relative intelligence of Negroes versus whites remains an insoluble issue. In those studies where certain factors which affect performance on I.Q. tests (e.g., parental education and social class) have been controlled, Negroes and whites score the same.[12] In Jackson, as the school board pointed out, Negroes perform less well on I.Q. tests than whites. Who would have suggested that they could perform equally, given their educational backgrounds? The Jackson tests did not, of course, control for socioeconomic factors.

Any discussion of biological differences between American whites and Negroes can hardly be taken seriously, since the genes of the two groups are so inextricably mixed. In any case, such presumed differences would not affect constitutional rights to an equal education.

rectly anticipated that these legal tactics would fail and that the crisis would finally be reached in late August.

The segregationists made their last-ditch plans. The governor convened a special session of the legislature to consider various actions designed to evade the law. After wrangling for days, the legislators passed a bill creating private schools. The bill provided $185 per year to help pay tuition for each white student who wished to avoid school desegregation. Another bill was passed to set up tests for students transferring within the previously existing school system to determine their grade assignment—an obvious authorization to punish Negro children who registered in white schools.

The legislature passed its new rulings in a fairyland atmosphere. Privately, the senators admitted that their school plan would not work. The U.S. Supreme Court was soon expected to declare unconstitutional a similar scheme in Virginia. In any case, the plan would have required $50 million a year to implement, $49 million more than the legislature had appropriated. The legislature's session went on in farcical fashion while the members played to the gallery, knowing quite well that their work was illegal. Indeed, a few who secretly disliked segregation even introduced amendments designed to make the new laws unconstitutional beyond a doubt. "It would have looked bad if we hadn't done anything," one senator said, "I don't think it will work anyway. I feel sure the Federal courts will strike it down. If they don't there's not enough money to make it work."

Less sophisticated people went about the state advocating the abolition of public education. The White Citizens' Councils assured their members that no education was better than integrated education, presumably consoling the parents in its ranks. In a "declaration of principle," the Jackson White Citizens' Council announced: "It is better to miss school altogether than to integrate. . . . [The council] will never retreat from its original position that there can be no compromise on the matter of integration." [13] The council said that it would finance private schools everywhere in the state. The Americans for the Preservation of the White Race also announced its intention of building schools for white children.

Despite the noise and fury, the segregationists' plan had collapsed by the end of August. Every city obeyed the courts' injunction to integrate peacefully. White children, despite the threat of boycott, attended the schools as usual.

On registration day in Jackson, forty-three Negro first graders entered eight previously all-white schools. Two neatly dressed six-year-old Negro boys walked up to the Galloway and Watkins schools in Jackson's north side and were politely enrolled. They were the first to break Mississippi's resistance.

Although somber-looking police glowered at the Negro children, integration came in peace. There were no shouting, cursing mothers as there had been in New Orleans, no federal troops as at Little Rock, and no killings as there had been at Oxford.

Some whites threatened violence when the schools actually opened their doors for the first day of classes. But, in early September when the schools started, integration came without bloodshed.

On the day that school opened in Biloxi, one could hardly have known that anything unusual was occurring. The streets of this city of 60,000 were empty when the Negro newcomers arrived at school. Twelve girls and four boys enrolled at four previously all-white elementary schools. At one school, Gorenflo Elementary School, four Negro youngsters, well-scrubbed for the big occasion, held hands around a pecan tree with their new classmates while playing a game. Soon, other Negro children applied for admission.

In Carthage (the hill town where KKK crosses had been burned in June), a lone Negro girl registered at the town's white elementary school on September 2. As the little girl, Debra Lewis, daughter of a farmer, walked into the school, she passed ranks of policemen. In addition to the town's regular police force, thirty-two auxiliary police, five sheriff's deputies, FBI agents, and nineteen U.S. Marshals guarded entrance to the school. Nine Negro children had intended to enroll in the white school where ex-Governor Ross Barnett had once been a student. But one by one, the families had received night visits from prominent businessmen issuing subtle threats. The visitors, in the words of Mrs. Minnie Boyd, told the Negro families: "You know, you don't *have* to send your child there."

Nor did official resistance end altogether. In Clarksdale, town officials rezoned the city to avoid even token integration. Unexpectedly, Negro children in Marks, Meridian, and Canton (towns which had not been subject to court orders) applied to enter white schools. School officials, sometimes physically barring the school entrances, turned them away. Eighteen Negro youngsters who tried to enroll in Jackson's white high schools also met with rejection.

Although it was clear that Mississippi would use every form of legal evasion and delay available, it was also clear that this last of the "bitter enders" finally had turned away from violent, total resistance to integration.

Why did at least token integration come with such unexpected ease? At least three reasons should be cited:

First, physical power backed up the law's enforcement with unmistakable intent. Federal marshals appeared at every school, and FBI agents (whose strength, rumors said, had been increased to five hundred men in August) were also in evidence. If a segregationist risked violence in the streets, he faced immediate punishment.

Second, the federal government made it plain that it would cut off school aid funds if Mississippi continued its intransigent policies. The Civil Rights Bill delegated to the U.S. Commissioner of Education the right to withhold aid funds from those states that refused to obey the law. However reluctantly, federal officials indicated in July that they would use the new powers. In a series of unpublicized workshops, men from the national government issued some politely stated but blunt threats. "We intend to follow the law," an Assistant Secretary of Health, Education and Welfare said, "and if that means cutting off all funds, then that's what will happen." [14] In a town like Biloxi, this would have been an economic disaster. The Biloxi school district has gotten $567,910 of federal funds to help in educating the children who came from adjacent Keesler Air Force Base. Confronted with a choice of remaining segregated or going it alone financially, Biloxi's leaders (like their fellow officials in the rest of Mississippi) apparently put their pocketbooks ahead of their segregationist principles.

A third factor which influenced the outcome, was the thorough preparatory work done by a moderate group called Mississippians for Public Education. Led by women, this extraordinary lobby group for integration talked many civic leaders into a campaign for peaceful compliance.

For the most part, Mississippi's state leaders kept their silence on the school issue out of either a desire to preserve racial peace or a fear that the school system would collapse financially. In contrast to rabble rousers like Ross Barnett, even Governor Paul Johnson told local communities "to resolve their own problems."

In Biloxi alone, thirty mothers affiliated with Mississippians for Public Education talked to some two thousand parents individually and in small coffee meetings. "We would talk to groups," said Mrs. Marge Curet, a mother who led the Biloxi campaign, "and take the position, 'If you want to . . . beat each other's brains out, that's all right with us. But when you catch *my* child in the middle, you've got a fight on your hands'." [15]

In Jackson, I talked with one of the harried leaders of the organization. We met in the rich neighborhood known as the country club section of Jackson, hardly the place where one would expect to find an underground opposed to the Mississippi "way of life." Yet, Mississippians for Public Education had all of the trappings of a clandestine revolutionary organization. A few of its

leaders, like Mrs. Gordon Henderson, wife of a sociology professor, allowed their names to be used publicly. Most of the members, like the woman with whom I spoke, had to remain
anonymous.

"Mrs. Grace Lloyd" typified the organization's membership.
College-educated, the wife of a rich lawyer, a socially prominent
woman, Mrs. Lloyd would normally have occupied herself with
bridge games and fashion shows. She had several children, however, who might have been affected by a school crisis. "When I
heard people talk about the schools, I began to be afraid," she told
me. "Our gardener sat down to have a beer the other day. He
casually said that he had bought $600 worth of ammunition for his
rifles. 'I'll stomp those niggers dead before they get in my boy's
school' was the way he put it. When I asked him if he would
actually kill a man, he replied, 'Sure, I'd kill a nigger. They aren't
human'."

Mrs. Lloyd joined the Mississippians for Public Education and
traveled extensively to organize branches in Oxford, Meridian,
Tupelo, Greenville, Biloxi, and Vicksburg. "At first, the going was
rough," she said. "People would talk seriously about how this or
that sheriff was a successful bootlegger and had not received an
education. They seemed to feel that closing the schools would be
no loss."

Mrs. Lloyd and hundreds like her reached many people in the
state. Their plea to keep the schools open won a response from
civic leaders, who, if not advocating their program, at least re-
frained from inciting mobs.

The White Citizens' Councils and the Americans for the Preser-
vation of the White Race roundly condemned women like Mrs.
Lloyd, calling them "as phony as their self-proclaimed motives."
The Lloyds had to withdraw the insurance on their house from a
Mississippi company and place it with an out-of-state firm, in fear
that it might be canceled as a reprisal for their activities. Both the
Lloyds and their children were threatened, and Mr. Lloyd felt

compelled to carry a gun in his car.

The efforts of the Mississippians for Public Education (backed by the physical and financial power of the federal government) finally gave Mississippi Negroes the victory they had been seeking for ten years. Only a hundred or so first graders benefited from this token move toward integration.* Yet the door had been opened. If federal pressure is sustained—and those who bravely took the first step survive—thousands more children will seize the opportunity for equal education.

The Freedom Party

In opening the public schools, the Negro cause won an unmistakable victory during the month of August, 1964. In another crucial area—assuring Mississippi Negroes participation in politics —COFO leaders scored a second, although more ambiguous, advance.

Early in 1964, a handful of Negroes had determined to create a new political party to mobilize the Negro masses. Even though voter registration held out a hope for the future, realistic observers knew that it might take a generation to form a really substantial Negro voting block. The Freedom Democratic party was conceived, therefore, as a unique "sham" party, an organization which would voice Negro protest and organize all those Negro citizens who had been denied direct political influence.

The plan, as it evolved by June, was simple: thousands of Negroes would enroll on freedom registration books, circulated by COFO workers. The new party would hold precinct meetings parallel to those of the regular Democrats; a platform expressing Negro grievances would be formulated; the party would then pre-

* The number was so small for two reasons: Many Negro parents feared for the safety of their children and, because of *de facto* residential segregation, white school boundaries do not normally include a large number of Negro families.

sent itself at the Democratic National Convention as the only Mississippi group loyal to liberal principles. Hopefully, the party might unseat the regular Democratic delegation, thus depriving the segregationists of the privileges and patronage derived from alliance with the national party.

Obstacles to this plan immediately became apparent. Only four people from the COFO headquarters (I was one) could be assigned to the task of actually organizing the 450,000 potential Negro voters in Mississippi. Further, most of the rural Negroes had little conception of the complicated machinery of precinct meetings and county committees, platform writing or convention challenges.

Basic educational work had to be undertaken at all levels. Workers trudged from door to door, gathering registration forms and patiently explaining the importance of the party organization. Other people conducted mock precinct meetings where Negroes ran through the laborious process of selecting chairmen, nominating delegates, moving and seconding motions—in a word, of practicing the fundamental democratic roles of our society. It was a painful process: people nominated themselves, the seconds failed to materialize, platform motions were phrased in the halting but haunting phrases of plantation workers. As one white observer who witnessed one of these meetings remarked: "You could feel the tension and the impatience and the frustration they felt in their ignorance, in front of white people who were in the audience. . . . They were full-grown adults who were participating, for the first time in their restricted lives, in the basic process of a free society. The light of pride in their faces showed through their embarrassment." [16]

The results came slowly, but by the middle of August approximately 80,000 people had registered on freedom ballots as members of the new party (the exact number is difficult to estimate since police raids resulted in the confiscation of unnumbered ballots). Precinct meetings took place in twenty-six counties and county meetings were held in thirty-five. Three hundred delegates, drawn from all parts of Mississippi, attended the party's first state convention in Jackson on August 6. They adopted a radical platform. Aside from pledging allegiance to the national Democratic party (a necessary step in securing recognition), the platform called for firm federal action to end discrimination in Mississippi. On a national level, Joseph L. Rauh of the Americans for Democratic Action effectively presented the new party's case to various delegations throughout the nation. By the end of August, ten state delegations to the Democratic National Convention had pledged to aid the Freedom party in its battle to unseat the segregationists.

The segregationists soon realized that the Freedom party constituted a genuine threat to the absoluteness of their control. On August 13, at the request of the attorney general of Mississippi, Chancery Court Judge Stokes Robertson banned the Freedom party and ordered its officers to stop functioning. The attorney general charged that the party "would cause irreparable damage to the public" and described it as a "conspiracy," "sham," and "fraud." It particularly irked the attorney general that one speaker of the Freedom party's state convention had described Mississippi as an "uncivilized" state. On August 22, the state government officially, and predictably, charged that the Freedom party was a Communist organization.

Some white men used stronger methods to ensure the Freedom party's defeat. On July 25, in Greenwood, whites beat up one party worker and threatened others. Police watched the incident. On July 26, in Hattiesburg, unknown assailants bombed the home of two party leaders with a "Molotov cocktail." On July 28, at Holly Springs, police surrounded a school where a precinct meeting was being held. The school superintendent had said he would burn down the school if a meeting took place. On August 11, in Ruleville, Mrs. Fannie Lou Hamer, a leader of the party, was again beaten in the county jail. On the same day, a white volunteer in Aberdeen was beaten while distributing freedom ballots. Police stood by and watched the beating. On August 12, in Oak Ridge, three carloads of masked men broke down the doors of homes housing Freedom party supporters. High-powered rifles were fired at the victims. On August 23, arsonists burned the Tupelo party headquarters.

Despite all the whites could do, the gigantic task of political education and organization went forward. Thousands of Negroes who had never known the nature of politics tasted its frustrations and rewards. By the end of August, a delegation headed by people like Aaron Henry and Ed King set off for Atlantic City, hopeful that their cause would receive recognition at the Democratic National Convention. A prime organizer of the party, Lawrence Guyot, had to remain behind. Guyot, chairman of the party's executive committee, had conveniently been jailed for thirty days just before the convention on a charge dating back to a protest demonstration in January.

The Freedom party presented Lyndon Johnson and Hubert Humphrey with a dilemma. Recognition of the party's status would satisfy the liberal conscience within the Democratic party but would irretrievably alienate white politicians in the South. Johnson, as an eminently practical politician, apparently felt that he could not afford such a loss. Yet a refusal to recognize the Freedom party's demand would constitute a moral abdication which northern Negroes and white liberals would be quick to recognize. President Johnson produced a compromise which, perhaps inevitably, failed to satisfy both the Freedom Democrats and their white southern opponents.

At first, President Johnson hoped to pacify the Negro delegation by some gesture such as granting them entrance to the convention floor, meanwhile requiring that the white Democrats pledge to open their state electoral processes to Negroes. The Freedom party immediately rejected this approach. "Negroes want Negroes to represent them," said COFO's Bob Moses. The white Mississippians, for their part, refused to grant any assurances about the future status of Negroes in the state.

A parade of witnesses went before the convention's credentials committee, testifying to the terror which deprived Mississippi Negroes of their rights. On the convention floor, Freedom party delegates (commenting "We have not been fighting in the underground for nothing") infiltrated the meeting and took over the seats of the white Mississippi delegation. Outside the convention, pickets mobilized by CORE and SNCC demonstrated in sympathy with the Negro cause.

Behind the scenes, Johnson called in Hubert Humphrey as a chief mediator. He suggested a compromise which the credentials committee eventually accepted: the white delegates would receive their places in the convention, but two members of the Freedom party group (Aaron Henry and Ed King) would also be seated. The Mississippi white delegation left the convention upon hearing the news. They left Atlantic City and returned to their homes. A month later, they vowed their formal loyalty to the Democratic party—they could not, after all, afford to lose their congressional seniority and the privileges that went with it. With hardly a single dissent, however, the white Mississippi Democrats announced their support of Senator Goldwater for President.

The Freedom party also decided to reject the Humphrey compromise. They reasoned that compliance would amount to a moral repudiation of their cause, an admission that whites legitimately ruled the state. As a result, they did not receive even token representation in the national Democratic party.*

Was this decision a serious mistake, a doctrinaire protest which

---

* An official Freedom party explanation of the decision justified the party's action in these words: "It must be understood that the FDP delegation did not come to Atlantic City begging for crumbs. They came demanding full rights, for themselves and for one million other human beings. They would have accepted any honorable compromise between reasonable men. The test was not whether the FDP could accept 'political realism,' but rather whether the convention and the national Democratic party could accept the challenge presented by the FDP. The convention and the national Democratic party failed that test."

frittered away some tangible gains? Joseph Rauh, the party's chief advisor, believed so and tried to argue the Freedom party delegates into treating the compromise as a victory. I am inclined to agree that the party's unbending dedication to principle accomplished little.

In spite of this tactical mistake, the Freedom party registered some important gains. Most significantly, the 1964 convention marked the end of all-white delegations from the South, for the convention passed a resolution stating that the proceedings of state Democratic parties must hereafter be open to all. If only two of the Freedom party's delegates were offered seats, it was still a triumph for a political group organized only four months previously. Mississippi was dramatically put on notice that the day of unchallenged all-white political rule in the state was coming to an end.

More positive results soon became clear. The Freedom Democrats returned to their state strengthened by a moral and symbolic triumph. Thousands of additional Negroes joined the party after August, and the group felt strong enough to present four congressional candidates and a senatorial candidate in the November elections on a "Freedom Ballot." In the future, the state's white politicians, if they wish to play any role at all on the national scene, will have to give nodding recognition to the wishes of Mississippi Negroes. Most important, the national Democratic party's traditional ties with the Jim Crow South have been cut once and for all. There is a good hope, although no assurance, that a really new order of equality is coming in southern politics.

A Balance Sheet

At the end of August, eight hundred of the summer volunteers headed back to their normal occupations as students or professors, lawyers or doctors. What had been accomplished? Had the deaths and bombings and a prospect of massive white retaliation been justified by tangible changes in Mississippi's way of life? Even the project leaders had difficulty in making a sure judgment. "Success?" Bob Moses responded to a reporter. "I have trouble with that word. When we started, we hoped no one would be killed." [17] And John Lewis, chairman of SNCC, had to admit, "We haven't opened a hole [in the Mississippi system] but we've made a dent." [18]

While the record was inevitably checkered, Mississippi would never be the same again. In a variety of crucial sectors, Mississippi society underwent tangible, and sometimes revolutionary, changes:

EDUCATION. Negro children peacefully entered public primary schools for the first time. While the vast majority of Negroes still had to attend inferior schools, the legal possibility of attaining an equal education had finally been secured.

The Freedom Schools initiated by COFO proved a solid success. In the future, most of the schools would continue on a permanent basis teaching such subjects as French, political science, and Negro history which the public schools lacked.

POLITICS. Between 1962 and 1964, 11,250 Negroes registered to vote. Approximately 2,150 of these enrolled during the summer of 1964.[19] This was a pitifully small increase: only 6.7 per cent of eligible Negroes were then registered to vote and, at this pace, it would take something over a hundred years to achieve full representation. Nevertheless, in the face of such unrelenting white resistance, even this advance (an increase of 75 per cent) testified to the courage and dedication of Mississippi Negroes. Further, the organization of the Freedom party gave the whites an unmistakable sign of the end of political apathy among Negroes. By establishing a network of active groups scattered around the state, by providing basic political education, by securing recognition from the national Democrats, the Freedom party made a healthy start toward mobilizing the Negro political potential.

LAW ENFORCEMENT. For the first time, many white Mississippians realized that they were not a law unto themselves. While the events of the summer cried out for more stringent action, the FBI arrests of a few whites who had molested Negroes—and most importantly, the detainment of Philadelphia's sheriffs—provided some hope that Negroes would be given protection under the law. Granted, it was only a hope; yet, as Bob Moses commented to *Newsweek* reporter William Cook, "The whole pattern of law enforcement of the past hundred years has been reversed. In some areas the police are offering protection where they never did before." [20] *

ACCESS TO PUBLIC ACCOMMODATIONS. In most of the larger towns, whites grudgingly opened their libraries and parks, their hotels and restaurants to Negroes. All did not go smoothly: Jackson closed its parks rather than integrate, Laurel shut its library, and Clarksdale shuttered most of its restaurants and hotels. Further, the rural areas had yet to be tested and, even in the "open" parts of Mississippi, most Negroes were still either too scared or too poor to use the facilities. Again, however, a beginning had been made. The solid wall of resistance had been cracked.

---

* The change in Mississippi's pattern of law enforcement needs to be put in historical perspective. Not so long ago, the killing of Negroes in Mississippi did not even require a public justification. Murder today demands that Mississippians use the resources of hypocrisy to excuse the action. The even more raw brutality of Mississippi at the turn of the century is described in an eye-witness account of a 1904 double lynching. One victim had been accused of murdering a white man. His wife was killed gratuitously. Here is what happened: "When the two Negroes were captured, they were tied to trees and while the funeral pyres were being prepared, they were forced to hold out their hands while one finger at a time was chopped off. The fingers were distributed as souvenirs. The ears of the murderers were cut off. Holbert was beaten severely, his skull was fractured, and one of his eyes, knocked out with a stick, hung by a shred from the socket. Some of the mob used a large corkscrew to bore into the flesh of the man and woman. It was applied to the arms, legs, and body, then pulled out, the spirals tearing out big pieces of raw, quivering flesh every time it was withdrawn."

COMMUNITY DEVELOPMENT. Twenty-three community centers located in rural areas were constructed during the summer. These centers (which were designed to continue in the future) attempted to serve basic needs: courses in nutrition and child care; library facilities; instruction in house-building, reading and writing, and industrial vocations; guidance in seeking the legitimate benefits provided by federal programs. Each of the centers contributed its small but significant victories toward the goal of changing the degraded condition of Mississippi Negroes.

MOBILIZING WHITE MODERATES. An unexpected result of the summer was that the white moderates learned they could exert considerable influence in the community. Working separately from COFO and from the Negroes, they succeeded in providing a relatively peaceful climate for acceptance of school integration and of the Civil Rights Bill. Despite the jibes of many northern liberals, the moderates finally showed their mettle. "If we can just hold our organization together," a Catholic priest told me, "we can establish a powerful economic and political base for change. For the first time, the moderates know their power—even though they still run scared."

A NEW EXPRESSION FOR NEGRO CULTURE. An intangible, yet stunning and vital result of the Negro revolt was the emergence of what some called a new "freedom culture." A "Caravan of Music" toured the state during the summer, its members singing and clapping and strumming the songs of revolt. As one observer put it, "History has never known a protest movement so rich in song." [21] The songs expressed the longings of Mississippi and gave people strength when times got tough. "Without these songs, you know we wouldn't be anywhere," Cordell Reagan, a freedom singer, told an audience in Greenwood. "We'd still be down on Mister Charley's plantation, chopping cotton for thirty cents a day." [22] The Free Southern Theater, another result of the movement, toured the state

with its production of "In White America." From Biloxi to Clarksdale, audiences responded enthusiastically to the simple, bitter pres-
entations. The repertory group was planned as a permanent addition to Mississippi Negro culture. In drama, in songs, in the poetry
written by freedom-school children, the Mississippi revolt produced additions to the Negro culture as unique and moving as jazz,
blues, or gospel preaching.

All of these changes from the burgeoning of Mississippi Negro
culture to the end of school segregation added up to an impressive
record of progress. Sometimes dramatically, sometimes with
tragic slowness, Mississippi *had* changed. Admittedly, no one
knows better than those who were there that these advances
were merely a beginning. As someone chalked on the wall
at COFO headquarters, "Lord, we ain't what we wanna be—
we ain't what we gonna be—but, thank God, we ain't what we
was." *

Clearly, what "we wanna be" would take many more years of
fighting and sacrifice to change into "what we gonna be." The
obstacles which lie ahead, and the course which has already been
traversed, can be traced in two Mississippi towns described previously: McComb and Greenwood. These little towns present hard-
core resistance to progress which reveals the depth of Mississippi's
problems. McComb is a Klan center where a freedom school began
to function in July of 1964. Greenwood, the scene of a violent
freedom day, is a farming village, long known for its defense of
segregation. Let us take a look at these towns once again, for they
represent in microcosm both the problems and the progress of the

---

* Much of the credit for the increased hope of Mississippi Negroes
must go to COFO and its workers. In describing the young volunteers,
Grenville Clark has rightly said, "They have brought some hope to hundreds of thousands of Negroes in the Deep South through demonstration by
deeds rather than by words that some at least of their fellow citizens are
concerned with the civil rights struggle. . . . They have furnished an
example of adherence to principle in the face of danger which must
inspire countless others. . . . Let them be recognized for what the are—
the true elite of our country." [23]

Mississippi revolt.

In McComb, the long, hot summer culminated in a series of explosions. At the end of July, whites bombed a local church as well as the home of a civil rights leader. On August 14, a supermarket across the street from the freedom school was blown up. On August 16, twenty-four policemen raided the COFO office, supposedly in a search for illegal liquor. They found none, but they carefully scrutinized literature and letters.

On August 23, hooded Klansmen abducted a white man who had befriended Negroes. Other whites who showed the slightest sign of sympathy for the civil rights movement suffered similar punishment. Mr. and Mrs. Albert Heffner, the parents of the 1963 "Miss Mississippi," had talked with some civil rights workers. As a result, they received three hundred abusive phone calls, cars of armed men circled their house, and finally they had to leave town.

On September 9, SNCC project director Jesse Harris requested help from the Justice Department's Civil Rights division. "We plead with you," he wrote, "to take action before it is too late." His letter drew no response from the government and, in fact, the number of FBI agents stationed in McComb dropped from sixteen to four.

On September 21, unknown attackers bombed a church and the home of Mrs. Aleyaenna Quinn, a Negro leader. Mrs. Quinn's two children were injured. These were the thirteenth and fourteenth bombings in the McComb area since the summer began. The police took no action except for arresting Mrs. Quinn's daughter on unspecified charges.

Mrs. Quinn had been active in the Citizens' League, a newly formed group of Negro business people who met secretly to aid civil rights activity. She owned a café which had been used as a meeting place for whites and Negroes. Police had raided the café twice, and her white landlord ordered her to close the restaurant. When she obeyed, he said: "Good, now I can go tell the sheriff and police chief and you won't be bombed." The loss of Mrs.

Quinn's business, however, was apparently not enough to satisfy the segregationists.

In response to the Quinn bombing, angry Negroes poured into the streets, roped off certain areas, and stoned police cars. Helmeted state police went into town and toured the Negro quarters in heavily armed groups. On September 22, 150 people came to a rally held on the site of the bombed church. For participating in the rally, police arrested five civil rights workers. Among those questioned, police interrogated Ursula Junk, an exchange student from Germany who had been working for COFO. Plainclothesmen, surrounded by McComb police, badgered the girl. They charged her with "inciting to riot."

"I have a right to call my embassy and have them provide a lawyer for me," Miss Junk said.

"When you enter Mississippi you ain't got no more rights," the detective told her, "didn't you know that?"

"I heard about that but didn't know it could be true."

"Unless you leave Mississippi voluntarily we are going to help you leave faster," the investigator told her.

"Do you date niggers?" another detective asked.

"I go out with people," she replied.

"You mean white people or niggers?"

The questioning went on in this vein. The policemen insinuated that Miss Junk was a prostitute. When they had established that she was a Catholic, one said, "Oh, those niggers climb on Catholics, too." [24]

The police submitted other workers to similar questioning. Eventually, the police released the five workers.

By the end of the summer, McComb whites had whipped themselves into a frenzy. Law and order in the town had completely broken down as the openly cynical police force aided the segregationists' attacks.

But this was not the whole story in the town. The whites had pushed the formerly docile Negroes to the wall until finally they fought back. Despite the bombings, the freedom school continued its operations. Local Negro businessmen donated land for a new community center. And on August 18, twenty-five potential Negro voters went to the courthouse to register during McComb's first "Freedom Day." (Only .006 per cent of the county's 35,000 eligible Negroes had registered, as opposed to 82 per cent of the minority whites.)

In September, the Negroes first used violent methods in repulsing white aggression. The riots on September 21 and 22 (a response to the bombing attack on Mrs. Quinn) made the whites realize that they could not endlessly continue their burnings and bombings with total impunity. This "backlash" from the Negroes pushed McComb to the brink of a violent revolution. Belatedly, but still courageously, several hundred white citizens of the town published a petition pleading for the maintenance of law and order.

Up in the Delta area, the town of Greenwood went through similar convulsions. In July, Negroes in the town had asserted their rights by registering to vote. In August, Negroes attempted to broaden their gains by testing access to public accommodations and by launching economic reprisals against the most brutal whites in the town. They met with great success in almost every endeavor. Voters streamed into the courthouse, children flocked to the freedom school, and the community center flourished. Formal "citizenship clubs" sprang up to press further for Negro rights.

These Negro advances stirred the wrath of Greenwood segregationists. Aided by the police, as in McComb, the white bigots intensified their attacks.

Negro families in Greenwood paid heavily for their bravery. Two Negroes, Annie Lee Turner and Silas McGhee, became the focal points of white anger.

In July Mrs. Turner, a young pregnant woman, had participated in Greenwood's "Freedom Day." For carrying a sign in a picket line, Mrs. Turner was tackled by police, hooked around the neck with a billy club, and dragged to a waiting police van. She suffered internal injuries. Other Negroes spotted the white man who had attacked her, a police officer named Henderson. They began a boycott of the store owned by Henderson.

The "selective buying campaign" which spread to the stores of other white men who had attacked Negroes during the registration drive provoked a series of incidents. On August 1, the police arrested two Negroes who participated in the boycott of Henderson's store. At the police station, the officer twisted one volunteer's arms behind him, kicked him, shoved his head three times against a concrete wall, hit him on the mouth with a stick, shoved and kicked him into a cell, kicked him seven more times after he fell to the floor, and then refused him a doctor.

On August 2, Annie Lee Turner was arrested again. Along with other Negro youths, she had been standing in front of Henderson's store. Henderson came, ordered them to disperse, and then dragged Mrs. Turner to a waiting police car. Other policemen (equipped with tear gas) set up a blockade around the store, anticipating Negro reprisals. After this incident, Mrs. Turner was a marked woman in Greenwood.

While her fate in the future remains uncertain (contrary to the usual historical accounts, Mississippi whites have often lynched Negro women), Mrs. Turner had not as yet received the punishment given to Silas McGhee and his family.

Silas McGhee's ordeal became a saga among Greenwood Negroes. In early July, McGhee as an individual tried to integrate a Greenwood theater. Whites at the theater beat him up. Later, FBI men arrested the attackers, using the power of the Civil Rights Bill for the first time.

Segregationists responded by shooting at McGhee's home on July 25 and by mobbing him on July 26, when he once again tried to enter a Greenwood theater. Although McGhee suffered serious injuries and was prevented for many hours from leaving Greenwood hospital by a blockade of armed whites stationed outside the building, he survived this attack without permanent damage. Police arrested him again on July 31 for driving with an improper vehicle license (in fact, his car had a valid Tennessee license plate). Police released McGhee on bond.

On August 15, his luck ran out. He was shot in the face by a white man who passed him as he was sitting by himself in front of a restaurant. The bullet entered his left temple and lodged near the left side of his throat. Friends rushed him to the McComb hospital. The doctors there said that they could not remove the bullet. Two men had carried McGhee into the hospital. The hospital staff refused them admittance because they were not wearing shirts. The men had taken off their shirts to help stop McGhee's bleeding.*

Not satisfied with what they had done to Silas McGhee, the Greenwood whites next attacked his family. On August 18, police arrested Jake McGhee, his younger brother, for an alleged traffic violation. When his mother, Mrs. Laura McGhee, went to pay the boy's fine, she was hit in the chest by the desk sergeant. Mrs. McGhee hit the officer in the nose. He went for his gun. Two COFO members held the policeman's hand until another officer came into the room and calmed him down. The police fined Jake McGhee a hundred dollars and issued a warrant for Mrs. Mc-

---

* The Mississippi medical profession is not well known for the quality of its mercy towards Negroes or towards white civil rights workers. Early in the summer, some northern physicians had requested Mississippi doctors to afford the same treatment to civil rights workers as they would to any other human being. Mississippi doctors, quoted in headlines in Jackson newspapers, piously affirmed their loyalty to the Hippocratic oath and viciously attacked the northern doctors. Yet, even a visitor in Mississippi could soon establish two facts: (1) In rural areas, Mississippi Negroes receive only the most casual treatment and only after they have waited for whites to pass ahead of them. Some hospitals are exempt from this charge. The University Hospital in Jackson seems to give quite equitable treatment, even though the city's Negroes accuse it of gross discrimination and prefer the Catholic hospital. (2) Some Mississippi doctors badly mistreat Negroes and civil rights workers. A case in point: On August 1, 1964, two civil rights workers, seeking treatment in a physician's office in Carthage, were severely beaten in the presence of Dr. A. L. Thaggard, who had refused to give them treatment. Dr. Thaggard, at the time of writing, carries on his humanitarian work in Carthage and continues as a respectable member of the AMA.

Ghee's arrest for assaulting an officer.

This was life in McComb and Greenwood, Mississippi, in the year 1964. In these enclaves of barbarity, shotguns and bombs had replaced the impartial rule of law. The petty tyrants imposed their will on pregnant women and defenseless men in ruthless fashion.

What will the future bring? Some observers believe that the silence of the "good people" and the connivance of police will allow barbarity to prevail indefinitely in Greenwood and McComb and Philadelphia. They think that the American people, however they may be temporarily lured from their moral lethargy by the spectacle of the murder of three young idealists, will in the end continue to allow Mississippi to follow its own ways of injustice and terror.

The more optimistic among us believe that the summer of 1964 was not just an episode or another futile, although admirable, exercise in American idealism. Rather, it could be the beginning of a new era in Mississippi—a time when the state's Negroes will shake off their apathy, a time when the civilized segment in the white community will take its stand against the mobs roaming the streets, a time when the federal government fulfills the promises which Lincoln made one hundred years ago.

Before we can draw up a prospectus for the future, we must comprehend the forces at work in Mississippi today: the bitter segregationists and the young Negro activists, the white "moderates" and the so-called "Uncle Toms." We must try to understand the convoluted Mississippi mind, for this is the first step in curing it. The state has, after all, produced people as different as William Faulkner and Ross Barnett, Richard Wright and the founder of the White Citizens' Councils.

5

The Mississippi Mind

"YOU all watch out now," the "Ole Miss" student said, almost giggling as he issued his threat, "you know what can happen to you if you get out of line." The student stood in front of the university's lyceum. A mob of other boys, perhaps twenty of them, urged him on, guffawing at his words. They had spotted my car with its suspicious California license plate just after I had entered the university campus. "Have you found any terrorism here?" the student asked. "Did you come to start trouble? Who invited you?" When foolishly and with more than a touch of cowardice I answered with the names of several professors, the student jeered, "I thought so! We know their type and we'll get them."

The threats sounded more ominous than usual for, if anywhere in Mississippi, one expected to find an oasis of reason in Oxford. Being trailed by police in Jackson, watching gunmen circle a farm in Carthage, seeing my car windshield smashed by Greenwood hoodlums—these seemed like predictable mishaps for a stranger

129

who came into a society rent with racial conflict. Yet, even while knowing the history of the "Ole Miss" crisis, I found it especially frightening to see this violent rabble still at work in the state's major place of higher learning.

Since the Meredith crisis, a feeling of fear had afflicted reasonable people in Oxford. One graduate student in history, JoAnn Bowman, had tried to rally student and faculty opinion against segregation. Burly students wearing football jerseys had tracked her around the campus, threatening her until she decided to leave the university. Professors reported that their offices had been rifled by night intruders. And the board of regents quite openly sought the dismissal of faculty members who voiced opinions contrary to Mississippi orthodoxy.

Perhaps even more disturbing than the outright lawlessness exhibited by a minority of students was the unwillingness or incapacity of the majority, who presumably were the future leaders of the state, to tolerate opinions different from their own. From childhood onward, these students had heard nothing but voices of indoctrination. As I talked with several advanced classes about "the race problem," I heard only boring repetitions of clichés from racist literature:

"Would you, as a father, wish your child to marry a Negro?"

"Niggers don't want change. They like things as they are."

"The Nigra caused the decline of Greece, Rome, Portugal, and Brazil."

"My father owns a plantation and the Negroes there are very happy. They're just lazy, irresponsible children."

Responding to the students was useless. They simply did not believe polls which reported that a great majority of Mississippi Negroes wanted desegregation, or evidence from intelligence tests showing the intellectual superiority of northern Negroes to Southern whites, or testimony about the Negro death rate in the state. For them the issue was closed: Negroes were innately inferior, "race-mixing" caused the decline of civilization and, therefore, the segregated system must be maintained forever.

A conversation with "Ole Miss" students quickly revealed why the state had so long been a center of terror and degradation. This social elite, embalming itself in rationalizations, had given up all responsibility for the misfortunes of Negroes. One could understand, too, why historian James Silver had to predict about his home state: "It would seem that for the foreseeable future the people of Mississippi will plod along the troubled road of resistance, violence, anguish, and injustice, moving slowly until engulfed in a predictable cataclysm." [1]

The intellectual elite at "Ole Miss" represents one segment of Mississippi society: a group determined to maintain segregation but usually unwilling to use violence. At the other end of Mississippi's social scale are the "white crackers," the farmers and small-town businessmen. Inspired by the righteousness of their cause, people of this type killed the civil rights workers, bombed homes, and burned a score of churches to the ground. They do the dirty work for the upper-class people who, while deploring the means and looking down on the "white trash," do not reject the ends.

The quality of the "cracker" mind was revealed to me one morning in a Carthage country store. Five white men sat on the run-down porch in front of the door. I had stopped to quench my thirst just as a busload of sailors pulled up at the crossroads. The sailors disembarked and then marched at a half-hearted pace down the nearby roads. Each carrying a stick to defend himself against snakes, the sailors had been charged with the duty of scouring the forest to find a trace of the missing civil rights workers. As the sailors dispersed, I listened to the white men talk, scoffing at the quest.

"They'll never find no bodies," a tall farmer said. "If there had been some bodies, the vultures would had told us by now. Probably those mealy students are down with Castro by now, just laughing away. It all smells to me like a plot by Kiddie Kennedy."

The rotund store owner, a man who evidently commanded respect from others on the porch, winked at the farmer and said, "No, you're wrong. You can bet they're out there some place with the chiggers chewing on their bones. They won't never be found 'cause those men from Philadelphia know how to do a job. They're deep down where they belong. They hadn't got no right comin' in here to cause trouble."

One old man, seeing that I was listening, wanted to know where I was from. When I replied, my apparently northern accent drew steely looks. "You hate us all up there, don't you?" he asked, rather pleadingly, "You just don't understand our niggers here like we do." I said I was ignorant on the subject and offered the old man a beer in return for enlightenment. "Well, son, first you got to realize what these niggers here are like. They're stupid as the day is long and too lazy to do anything except get their welfare check. They'll cheat you if you turn your back, cut you when they're drunk, and slaver after your women. Why we done 'em a favor, taking 'em out of Africa where they ate each other. Sometimes they is good but sometimes they gets smart with us and we got to teach 'em a lesson." A truck drove up and a Negro asked the store owner's wife for gas. The aproned fat woman responded politely enough, smiled and called, "Goodbye George," after the man had paid.

"There goes a good nigger," the old man continued, "but these young'uns don't know their head from a watermelon. In the old days we knew how to treat this kind that thinks they're so good. Why, in '16, I remember how thousands gathered in town to see one of these black rapists roasted. We toasted him over a fire till he really squirmed. Mark you," he said, pointing a stubby finger at me, "we'll fight for our freedom."

"You guys up North think you can put things over on us," one of the other farmers joined in, "but we know what's happening. All those Commies and the UN and Earl Warren are trying to get us conquered by them Russians and Africans. You want some woolly-headed nigger with his white sluts to boss over our state."

The old man broke in as the other farmer became more excited. "Those niggers are probably just tools, they is too dumb to know what's going on. We'll treat 'em the way they expect. Food, drink, and women, that's all they need."

When I failed to argue with the men, their anger dissipated. They talked again of their crops and of a baseball game between an Indian team and whites. They returned to their secluded mental universe, clutching to those myths which gave them some dignity. Wherever one went in Mississippi, one found whites repeating the same theme: "We're better than the niggers," "We treat them well," "We punish the ungrateful," "We will fight against evil influences from the outside world." Like paranoids, Mississippi whites viewed themselves as innocent, heroic victims of a subversive plot. Theirs was a small, frightened world, bordered on one side by a black devil and on the other by a white God who assured them of their worth. One has to understand this mythology before comprehending how Mississippians can condone murder and still live with themselves.

What the Mississippi White Believes

In order to justify his closed society, the average Mississippi white subscribes to four central beliefs: the Negro is inferior, a Communist plot menaces the white system, God sanctions white supremacy, and the Mississippian's personal ethics come before manmade law. With varying emphasis and more or less sophistication, the white man weaves these beliefs into a coherent apologia.

The keystone of the white ideology is, of course, the conviction that fate has sanctioned Negro inequality. Rejecting all southern history from the slave chain gangs through the lynching period, the average white believes that nature, not nurture, has produced the often diseased, often ignorant, and always poor southern Negro. William Brink and Louis Harris, after conducting an extensive poll, have detailed the usual stereotyped views which the southern white holds about Negroes.[2] Over 80 per cent of whites believe that Negroes are lazier than whites, have a peculiar odor, and adhere to looser morals. About 60 per cent believe that Negroes wish to live off the handout, are messy, prone to crime, and have less native intelligence.

The most deep-seated prejudice is that Negro males wish sexual relations with white women. This belief causes the most fear and anger in the white man, and no amount of contradictory evidence can dispel it. Its subconscious sources are difficult to fathom, but presumably it derives from the white man's own guilt about his sexual actions. Since every Negro in Mississippi today has at least one white ancestor (see p. 107) due to the liaisons maintained by white masters and slave women, the amount of "race-mixing" has obviously been great.

Whatever the amount of Negro blood in their own ancestry, whites believe that the shiftless, stupid, lecherous, violent Negro is a lower animal deserving pity or ridicule but hardly respect. Thus, if the white man establishes schools for Negroes or gives them jobs, he is being charitable and kind, for the Negro really deserves nothing. Picturing himself as a kindly benefactor, the white naturally expects that the Negro should love him. And strangely enough, most whites really do think that Negroes have kindly feelings towards them. Letters to Jackson newspapers continually exhibited this conceit.

"Here where I live we have always treated our colored friends good," a fifteen-year-old girl wrote in an "open letter" to President Johnson, ". . . and they love us. . . . I have enjoyed complete freedom up to now because I knew our colored friends loved me." [3] A Mr. Howard Bartling, in another letter, wrote: "I have a lot of good Negro friends and my flesh crawls and I almost get sick to my stomach when I think of how lousy reporters and agitators have tried in every way to take away the Southern Negroes' happiness. . . ." [4]

Blending a belief in their own goodness with a conception of Negro contentment, the whites have been genuinely surprised at the Negro revolt. They can attribute it only to the Negroes' stupidity and, most importantly, to the prodding of outsiders. A supposedly humorous blasphemy of the Twentythird Psalm, published in the *Jackson Daily News,* expresses this white indignation at "foreign" influences:

Martin Luther King's Version of the 23rd Psalm

Lyndon B and Bobbie are my shepherds; I shall not want.
They maketh me to lie down in front of white theaters.
They leadeth me into white universities.
They restore my welfare checks.
Yes, 'tho I walk through the heart of Dixie, I shall fear no police, for Bobbie is with me.
His tear gas and paratroopers, they comfort me.
They anointeth my head with hair straightener,
My gas tank runneth over.
The Supreme Court and Urban League shall follow me all the days of my life and I shall dwell in the Federal housing forever [sic].

This litany of evil influences—the President, the Attorney General, the Supreme Court—is chanted continuously in the state's newspapers. Lurking behind them, supposedly, is an intricately conceived Communist conspiracy. Clearly, the whites need some scapegoat, for otherwise they could not explain why the Negro had suddenly turned against them. Incredible as it may seem, many whites truly believe that Communist agents have caused their troubles.

"Communists are not just 'involved,' in these demonstrations—they are behind it and have been planning such moves for years," one writer in a Mississippi newspaper said, responding to skeptical comments by a University of North Carolina professor. "Furthermore," he informed the professor, "it is not without cause, that the University of North Carolina is known as the 'Red Nest'; nor is it deniable that its Philosophy Department is so infiltrated that at one of its meetings, it asked the audience to stand during the playing of the Communist 'Internationale'." [5]

This feeling that they are victims of a widespread plot afflicts many Mississippi whites. A Ku Klux Klan pamphlet declares: "The people whom we have elected to run the affairs of this nation are either very stupid or have joined a conspiracy to sell us all out, and that is a fact!" [6] A spokesman for the White Citizens' Councils said, "An all-out war is being waged against the white race." [7] And in 1964, the most popular publication in Mississippi was *Color, Communism and Common Sense,* a John Birch publication "revealing" Communist influences in the Negro population.[8]

In their presumed battle against "Communist integrationists," the whites comfort themselves with the assurance that God is on their side. He is not a soft, kindly God but rather, in the Baptist view, a God of anger, firm judgment, sternness, and revenge. His representative in Mississippi is the Baptist church, an institution which comes close to having an established status. In the most churchgoing state in the nation, religion naturally plays an important role in all aspects of life. And in Mississippi, the Baptist church has thrown all its weight behind the fight to preserve segregation. In 1964, for example, the state convention of the Democratic party was, as usual, opened by an invocation from a Baptist minister. He announced, among other things, that segregation was God's will, that God supported the free enterprise system, and that God liked the southern way of life.

The most popular religious radio program in Mississippi, "The Christian Beacon," parrots segregationists views. In interpreting the Book of Revelations, for example, "The Christian Beacon" leads its followers to believe that "A great beast—that is, world government—is trying to control us and make us all think with one mind. This beast is trying to get our church socials integrated." Not long after the University of Mississippi riots, the Mississippi Baptist Convention defeated several resolutions testifying to "our intelligent good will toward all men" and refused to approve a prayer "that we will live consistent with Christian citizenship." [9]

From childhood onward, the white person learns that God favors segregation. The White Citizens' Councils, for example, suggest the following reading for third and fourth graders:

> God wanted the white people to live alone. And he wanted colored people to live alone. . . . We must keep things as God made them. . . . Negroes use their own bathrooms, they do not use the white people's bathroom. The Negro has his own part of town to live in. This is called our Southern Way of Life. . . . God has made us different and God knows best.[10]

With God on their side, whites need have little fear of divine retribution for their behavior. Indeed, their fight for segregation takes on the dimensions of a holy war. When this atmosphere of righteous indignation is allied with a spirit of anarchism, as it is in many Southerners, violence comes easily. Perhaps because of their religious tradition—a culture which encourages personal revelation and disdain for authority—the white people of the state have cultivated a blithe disrespect for the law. On important matters (dealing with the "nigger," protecting personal honor, drinking), the typical white believes that no authority supersedes his individual convictions. This atmosphere of anarchism makes it easier for Mississippians to refuse to be bound by the national will. It allows them to promulgate one law for themselves and another for Negroes. And it creates such anomalies as these:

—While officially the state subscribes to a Baptist doctrine of teetotaling, the government collects a sizable tax from the sale of liquor. Approximately one million dollars a year comes into state coffers from this tax on a legally prohibited product. In the larger counties, sheriffs are reported to receive up to $100,000 annually for "protection."

—While the state proclaims itself as peaceful and contented (officials proudly cite its generally low crime rate), Mississippi is tied with Alabama in having the highest incidence of violent crimes, assault and murders, in the nation. It is the only state in the union where forest fires are more often started by arsonists than by accident.

—While its senior senator publicly describes Mississippi as offering the finest education, the state spends less per capita on education than any other in the union. Its school officials (while applying for federal funds) reported 60,000 more pupils in 1950 than the U.S. Census had counted.

A debonair disregard for the truth, lawlessness allied with righteousness, and a contempt for Negroes are the major elements which go into the making of the Mississippi mind. Mississippi spokesmen have woven these strands into an elaborate ideology justifying the southern way of life. Various organizations in the state, from the Klan through the State Sovereignty Commission, disseminate this ideology and ensure that schools, pulpits, and the press—potential sources of deviation—reflect the orthodox view.

Conformity in Mississippi is not left to chance but is rather a matter of careful planning by several powerful institutions. No single organization has greater importance as a molder of white opinion than do the White Citizens' Councils. The councils both reflect the white view and, when necessary, manipulate public opinion by electoral or economic pressure. It was the councils that crushed the integration movement in Yazoo City with a boycott, that blacklisted professors at "Ole Miss," and that forced liberal newspapers out of business. At one time or another, the councils have listed as subversive organizations the Red Cross, the Air Force, and the Young Women's Christian Association. Legislators have publicly testified to their fear of countering the councils' line, and teachers know that their livelihood depends on conformity. "We are in a tight bind," a high official at the University of Mississippi told me, "the federal government is about to cut off our grants and the White Citizens' Councils get the legislature to chop our budget whenever a professor opens his mouth or a new Negro student comes to the university."

The White Citizens' Councils have two leaders who forged their policies: Senator James Eastland, their "patron saint," and William J. Simmons, their organizer. When the Supreme Court handed down its school decision, Senator James Eastland soon emerged as the loudest proponent of white supremacy. In setting policy for the White Citizens' Councils, Eastland's words have become gospel: "There can be no outcome but total and complete victory . . . the law of nature is on our side . . . the drive for racial amalgamation is both illegal and immoral." Quite openly, Eastland has talked of how disregard for the law will cripple integration moves. As chairman of a Senate committee that reviewed all civil rights laws, for example, Eastland has wide sway. "They said that I broke the law. And so I did," he once admitted. "You know what happened? Why, for the three years I was chairman, that committee didn't hold a meeting. . . . I carried those bills around in my pocket everywhere I went, and every one of them was defeated. The CIO and these racial groups yapped and yapped. But their yapping didn't get them anywhere." [11]

While Eastland does the talking (and continues, as chairman of the Senate Judiciary Committee, to impede civil rights legislation and to select Mississippi's federal judges), William J. Simmons handles the task of building the White Citizens' Councils into a unified, powerful organization.

Simmons, a native Mississippian, serves as national administrator of the White Citizens' Councils. During the regime of Governor Ross Barnett, Simmons acted as a "prime minister for racial integrity." As one astute observer described Simmons in 1964: "This suave, sophisticated zealot was ready to prove himself a genius at indoctrination on a massive scale. He was to call the tune in interpositions, direct the unpledged electors in 1960. . . . His outfit, the White Citizens' Councils, would henceforth receive a generous slice of the state funds ($160,000 by the summer of 1963) allotted to the Sovereignty Commission." [12] Simmons, as the intellectual of segregation, reworked the doctrines of Gobineau, William Henry Chamberlain, and Goebbels into a new paean to the white "race."

I met Simmons in 1964 in the White Citizens' Councils offices which conveniently fronted on the governor's mansion in Jackson. Reaching him proved difficult, since a bevy of secretaries guarded him ("I assume you are a white man," one of them said over the phone after arranging an appointment. "I would have to cancel the date if you aren't.") Simmons's office contained outdated books on Negro intelligence, several dictating machines, and a mass of small Confederate flags. In one corner lay some packed luggage. Simmons was about to take off for Chicago and Los Angeles, organizing new branches of the White Citizens' Councils there. Apparently, the charge of acting as an "outside agitator" did not disturb him. Simmons proved to be a smooth, loquacious man, a southern Baptist, a brother in Kappa Alpha fraternity, member of the Kiwanis Club and Jackson Chamber of Commerce. Head of the Jackson Citizens' Council since its inception, Simmons told me in pseudo-scholarly terms about the organization's cardinal principles:

"Integration has proved that it does not and will not work," he argued. "Segregation is not the result of starry-eyed idealism unrelated to facts. It is based on *truth*." The essential truth for Simmons was that Negroes are innately inferior, an assumption which he tried to prove by citing whatever scholarly authorities he could muster on his side. "Psychological tests always show the Negro to be inferior," he maintained. Like less sophisticated Southerners, Simmons shared the belief that Negroes really preferred the segregated system. "I don't put any credence in these reports about voting. The Negroes I know are happy. They are just embarrassed by this so-called 'civil rights' movement." He added, as an afterthought, "After all, voting is a privilege, not a right."

Whether genuinely or not, the White Citizens' Councils leader appeared to believe that white men suffered from the effects of a worldwide conspiracy against them. "The integration drive in the United States is openly allied with the nationalist campaign in

Africa to obliterate the white man," he mentioned, hinting at a devious conspiracy.

When asked about the White Citizens' Councils' influence, Simmons dismissed it lightly: "Why I just laugh when I hear this stuff about Bill Simmons making legislators jump. No man can get them to do that. As for economic reprisals, there may have been some but it was all spontaneous. . . . Anyway, you should talk to our chief of police in Jackson about how some Negroes put on pressure to enforce a boycott of downtown stores."

Simmons exuded confidence about the future: "We are expanding into the North and West. . . . No one will obey the Civil Rights law . . . resistance will harden to the Supreme Court decision. . . . In any case, Goldwater will carry the South and undoubtedly the nation." In fact, an incredible 87 per cent of Mississippi's registered voters cast their ballots for Goldwater in 1964.

Simmons laced our conversation with his own brand of jokes. "Justice Hugo Black used to wear a white robe to frighten blacks," he said while commenting on the Supreme Court, "now he wears a black robe to terrorize whites." At times he would utter a witty aphorism: "Integration is that period between the arrival of the first black and the departure of the last white."

Behind the smiling façade, one could easily see a man of depth and power, dedicated for whatever reason to maintaining white supremacy. Under his guidance, the White Citizens' Councils (allied with similar organizations) had, as one writer put it, "created a climate of fear that has strait-jacketed the white community in a thought control enforced by financial sanctions, and has undone most of the improvements in race relations made over the last thirty years." [13]

One would think that few native whites would challenge the Mississippi system of belief and the institutions which support it. Sterilized by propaganda and intimidated by organized pressure, such as that coming from the White Citizens' Councils, most white men do indeed conform, Some Mississippians, however, break away from the majority and try to defend a more sane attitude toward race relations. Their numbers are difficult to estimate, for most of them have to work clandestinely. Some white people who are active in civil rights programs estimate there are only thirty actual leaders among the moderates—and some of these will not publicly take a stand. These quiet rebels against the system counted a variety of people in their ranks: businessmen and professionals, housewives, priests, and a few farmers. They deserve attention since the South's future may well depend on their unpublicized activities.

The White Moderates

When a national commentator called Paul Johnson a "moderate," the Mississippi governor indignantly went before television cameras to repudiate the charge. His response typified Mississippi's way of thinking. The term "moderate" has come to signify a weak-kneed person who gives in to federal tyranny in the most cowardly fashion. Nevertheless, while most whites consider moderation a vice and punish it with ostracism or worse, signs of dissent still appear in the closed society.

Mississippi women, who perhaps take their religion more seriously than the men, are at times the most vociferous critics of the state. An elderly housewife, for example, publicly chided her fellow citizens for their neglect of justice. "Local and state officials have encouraged the white man with his murderous heart to kill and mistreat the Negro," Mrs. A. J. Noel of Jackson said in July, 1964. She pleaded with her fellow Mississippians to stop the killings and beatings, and to treat the Negro with a semblance of justice.[14]

Another woman, who had been raised in Mississippi and had attended the university, wrote her home-town newspaper, "What in heaven's name is going on in my home state these days?" Mrs. Bruce Cooper had temporarily moved to Virginia and found that integration was not as horrible as she had been taught. "True, when my husband and I first moved North, we felt uncomfortable eating in integrated restaurants . . . but after a while, we ceased to notice. We have met several well-educated, well-mannered, well-dressed, thoroughly nice Negroes who have become—if not friends—at least close acquaintances." She touched too on the intermarriage stereotype, "I have absolutely no fear that either of my children will marry a Negro, simply because they have met Negroes at school. . . . Yet how could I deny children the permission to marry persons they loved?" She concluded ruefully, "I still stand up when a band plays 'Dixie,' but I'm not sure I can much longer." [15]

Many people in Mississippi share these sentiments. Public opinion polls have shown that a majority of Southerners (and a large minority of Mississippians) are willing to assure Negroes their legal rights. Of those answering a recent poll, 88 per cent believe, for example, that Negroes should be allowed to vote, 80 per cent say that Negroes should have equal job opportunities, and 45 per cent would not even object to school desegregation. Yet only 31 per cent of southern whites would favor legislation backing up the Negro's right to vote.[16] This disjunction between what they say they believe and what they are willing to do paralyzes men of good will in the South and especially in Mississippi. "There are fine, good people in this state—many of them," editor Ralph McGill has commented about Mississippi. "They are here but they are not running the government. The 'good people' are not represented. . . . God help us." [17]

Common sense, caution, fear, cowardice—call it what you will —prevent most of Mississippi's "good people" from doing anything to change their society. Many of the state's big businessmen, professionals, ministers, and professors privately deplore the atmosphere of terror, yet they cannot muster the courage to combat it.

The social elite in Mississippi affirms its good will and protests its innocence. It has great power economically and as a molder of public opinion but seldom uses its influence for the public good.

One contractor spoke out against racial prejudice in a laymen's society meeting at his church and had even allowed his wife to serve on an interracial community committee. "Then we began to get the telephone calls," he remembered. "People would call us at all hours and say the most vicious things to my wife. Some companies canceled contracts. My biggest worry was over a highway contract I was about to sign with the state. I was told—in an indirect way, to be sure—that I would lose the contract if my wife did not quit that committee. She quit." The contractor evidently felt some qualms about his subsequent silence on the racial issue. "I don't like these roughnecks who cause all the trouble. I don't like the cops. But what can I do about them? You wouldn't want me to lose my business, would you?" He added in a self-righteous tone, "Who would feed my children?"

A well-known Jackson lawyer had gone somewhat further than the contractor. He had signed a petition which advocated that public schools should be kept open even if Negro children entered, a quite radical position in Mississippi. "We got the consequences right away," he said. "The neighbors won't talk to us and their children throw stones at our kids. I'm scared stiff. I keep a rifle in the house and a pistol in the car." The lawyer was an old-family Mississippian who had received his college education in the North. "Gradually I just gave up all this nonsense about Negroes, but most of my old school friends, having never left the state, still think of Negroes the way I did." While he personally was kind to Negroes, he never invited one to his house. "That wouldn't do them any good and it would be bad for me." Signing the petition had been his one act of public defiance. "After this, however, I'm going to keep my mouth shut. The big lawyers around here are all for segregation—we've even got an ex-president of the American

Bar Association in the city who calls the Supreme Court decision illegal. I can't buck that." He settled back comfortably to enjoy our after-dinner liquor. From the luxurious vantagepoint of his library, one could hardly picture the civil rights workers lying in state jails for lack of legal counsel.

Ministers and professors might seem the logical voices of conscience, but in Mississippi they have quietly abdicated their responsibilities. Most ministers feel that an occasional guarded sermon about loving one's fellow man discharges their obligations. As for professors, one of them gave a typical apology for his colleagues at a meeting of sociologists: "We can't really say anything. Young men without tenure would lose their jobs and old men would lose their pensions. We *really* have academic freedom at my university but we know that responsibility goes with freedom, so we use it discreetly. Our problem is how to preserve the higher educational system—the only hope of our state—while pleasing the politicians." Although he knew better, the sociologist tried to preserve his self-respect by pointing to Negro advances. "Why, they really aren't so badly off. Maybe they just need to work harder. We've given them good schools and other facilities." Later, on a drive around his university town, he pointed to a dirty field and said proudly: "We even gave them that as a park."

The intellectual and social elite in the state does have a difficult problem, for its members would suffer various kinds of punishment if they took a stronger stand. Then, too, its members worry about whether they can be more effective "within" rather than "outside" the system. Up to a point, a legitimate argument can be made that a civic leader can have more influence as, say, an elected official than he can as an outright critic rejected by most of his fellow citizens. In Mississippi, however, the white moderates have let tactful caution turn into cowardice. On a variety of critical issues—school integration, the Oxford crisis, legal neglect of civil rights workers, violence against Negroes—they have kept silent. Their absence from the field has almost always given segregationists an easy victory.

In the summer of 1964, when moderate groups took the unprecedented step of urging that the Civil Rights Law be obeyed and public schools kept open, they were surprised at their own power. Rather than being exiled, the more vocal moderates in the social elite found that many in the community would follow them. Even so, in 1964, the moderates did not act on their own initiative but were pushed by federal law, federal power, national public opinion, and by the Negro revolt. As a "reserve force"—a group which can be called into action in certain situations to exert the final push forward—the moderates can be very useful. But the initial, most important impetus for progress will still have to come from Negro leaders, from federal decisions or . . . just possibly, from a small group of white radicals who have been lampooning Mississippi orthodoxy.

The White Radicals

A handful of brave whites have fought with consistency and bravery to change the Mississippi way of life. In the confusing Mississippi vocabulary, some might go by the political label of "socialist" while others would call themselves "conservative." Unanimously they reject the myths which sustain segregation. They want equal schooling, equal justice under the law, and equal protection from violence. And unlike the moderates, they have been willing to suffer the economic and physical hardships which are the reformers' lot in Mississippi.

As a group, the radicals have few characteristics in common. Perhaps because their position requires unusual bravery, even streaks of eccentricity, stubbornness, and humor, they can be described only in their own terms as individuals. David Minter, a doctor, and Eugene Cox, a farmer, used to run the Providence Farm near Tchula; P. D. East edited a weekly newspaper in Petal and Hattiesburg; Ed King serves as the chaplain at Tougaloo College; James Silver is a professor of history at "Ole Miss," and Hazel Brannon Smith publishes several Mississippi journals. These six people represent the quite different ways that white radicals participate in the opposition as well as the quite common penalties they suffer.

David Minter, a highly respected country doctor in Holmes County, lived in Mississippi since the 1930's. Together with Eugene Cox, he ran a cooperative farm. Originally, the two came to Mississippi to establish a religious utopia. The vicissitudes of the depression frustrated their plans, and in 1955, Providence Farm consisted of Dr. Minter's clinic, a camp for Negro children, a credit union for tenant farmers, and some dusty acres.

Minter and Cox had adjusted to Mississippi life and no longer regarded themselves as reformers. They attended a local church, made friends with the whites, and deviated from local custom only in treating Negroes as their social equals. This was enough, however, to provoke an attack from their fellow townsmen.

In October of 1955, when four Negro boys who lived near the Providence Farm whistled at a white girl, police hauled them in for questioning about Minter and Cox. The chairman of three local White Citizens' Councils set up a tape recorder to catch the boys' testimony. When the Negroes said that Cox and Minter held integrated meetings at the farm and talked of the Supreme Court, the whites called a secret town meeting for the next night. There, the tape was heard again by five hundred white men. The climactic point of the evening came when Eugene Cox, who had been watching the meeting from the back, got up and said that he believed segregation was un-Christian. With only two negative votes, the county's citizens decided to expel the Minter and Cox families.

For a while, the two nonconformists attempted to carry on their business. And some townspeople, perhaps feeling remorse the morning after, spoke to them as if nothing had happened. One man who had said that "What we need tonight is a couple of grass ropes" returned to friendly relations with them. The local insurance companies, however, canceled their policies and the sheriff (who had played a leading role as a prosecutor at the meeting) set up a guard to search cars entering the farm. When threats against his and Minter's children accumulated, Cox sat up for ten nights straight holding a rifle. They stuck it out until 1956, when both families fled the state.

The townspeople had all liked the Minters and the Coxes, but when it came to racial issues they felt that a line had to be drawn. "They were practicing social equality out there," Edwin White, a lawyer and White Citizens' Councils leader said in 1956, and he added pleasantly, but with unveiled meaning, "We won't have it." [18]

While the Coxes and Minters tried to combat segregation with Christianity, P. D. East used humor. East, a native-born Southerner, had started his newspaper, *The Petal Paper,* as a typical small-town journal. He carried the weekly news of Hattiesburg and Petal along with the usual short features, such as "Citizen of the Week" and "Prayer and Meditation." He had joined the local civic clubs, condemned sin in his editorials and, as he later wrote: "I glad-handed from hell to breakfast, winning friends and conning people." He carefully avoided mentioning the race issue. While the paper prospered, East's conscience began to trouble him. "When I'd become aware of my state of mind, I would be frightened and snap back with a healthy smile and a hearty handshake. Such is the effect of the sweet smell of money." [19]

After the Supreme Court decision of 1954, East could no longer tolerate acquiescence to the southern mystique. He began to write biting articles, attacking the southern way of life. His editorials sought a restoration of justice and law in the South. For example, he questioned a bill the legislature had passed which donated state funds to the White Citizens' Councils. He wondered about the fairness of using tax money collected from Negroes to support an organization whose only purpose was to harness them in their servitude. East attacked another law which would have imposed fines on integrated churches, calling it a direct violation of constitutional protections for freedom of religion. In 1956, when he learned that the Citizens' Councils were about to start a local branch, East carried an advertisement in his paper which announced:

> Suh,
> Here's Sweet Music,
> Yes, YOU too, can be
> *SUPERIOR*
> Join the Glorious Citizen Clan
> Next Thursday Night!

The advertisement asked readers to "compare these 10 Freedoms" with other "Old-Fashioned Offers": "Freedom to interpret the Constitution of the United States to your own personal advantage! Freedom from worry and fear if you happen to set before a jury! Freedom to be superior without brain, character or principles! . . ." He added, "Remember: Not to join could mean you're a Nigger-Lover!" [20]

East never let his readers forget the plight of Mississippi Negroes. When his town completed a sparkling new white school, East published a picture of it alongside a dilapidated Negro school; he asked the readers to identify which was which. When whites beat up local Negroes, East formed a "Bigger and Better Bigots Bureau." He pleaded that whites and Negroes should "sit down as human beings with mutual problems and with mutual respect to begin to work out differences." [21]

East reserved some of his sharpest comment for southern politicians who yelled "nigger" the loudest. Senator James Eastland, whom East irreverently called "Our Gem," did not escape criticism. "In addition to his character, his integrity, and his principles," East wrote, "Our Gem is not only intelligent in the usual manner, but he's sharp as a tack in other ways. Example: At

Doddsville, Mississippi, Our Gem has a small cotton patch, composed of something like 5,020 acres. And in the United States Senate, who has been the strongest fighter for the cotton farmer? Of course, our very own cool cat." [22]

Mississippi could not stand these criticisms of her most sacred idols. East found his subscriptions and ads dropping off sharply. He was cut off by most of his friends. His children had to play by themselves. Over the telephone, people called him a "goddam Nigger-loving, Jew-loving, communist son-of-a-bitch." He began to carry a gun. He had hoped that people in his community might tolerate an outspoken newspaper. When it became clear that they wouldn't, East later said: "My reaction was as it had been before and as it was to be many times, in days to come. I was depressed to the point that I went into my room at home, sat on the side of the bed and wept like a baby." [23] Somehow, East escaped violent physical attack, although some whites made half-hearted attempts to intimidate this 220-pound man. One day, when he stopped his car at a red light, a white man walked up and demanded: "Get outta that car, so's I can mop up the street with you." East said "Sorry, pal, that ain't enough inducement," and pulled his car away.[24]

Economic reprisals began to hurt and, by 1964, it appeared that East's paper had gone bankrupt. Even while sinking into economic ruin, he kept on writing. He was a man "living at his lowest and writing at his highest," as one friend described him, "a grief-stricken man who turns out monstrously funny copy. Like Monoculus, he poked fun at the devil." [25]

Hazel Brannon Smith, another newspaper editor, has also exhibited unusual courage in fighting against injustice. Since 1936, Mrs. Smith has edited the Lexington weekly newspaper in Holmes County; more recently, she started to publish the *Northside Reporter,* a Jackson newspaper.

In 1954, Mrs. Smith began a battle with Sheriff Richard Byrd of

Holmes County. In July of that year, Byrd, while cruising around town, passed a group of Negroes. He told them to disperse and beat one of them to make sure that they got the message. As they ran away, the sheriff shot another boy, Henry Randle. As the Negro lay wounded, the sheriff returned to his car and drove on.

After investigating the incident, Mrs. Smith found that Randle had been in town to buy food and had never been involved in a crime. "I wouldn't defend a trouble-maker," she said later, "but it seemed to me that the whole future of race relations down here depends on our protecting our good citizens. . . . I thought a long time and then decided that, if I didn't print this story, I was just as guilty of shooting that Negro as Richard was." [26]

She printed a front-page editorial. "The laws in America are for everyone—rich and poor, strong and weak. . . . This man was shot in the back. He was running only because he had been told to 'get going' by the sheriff. . . . He just made the one mistake of being around when the sheriff drove up." [27]

The sheriff sued her newspaper. Mrs. Smith's husband was fired from his job, and the Citizens' Councils saw to it that the newspaper lost many of its advertisements. But Mrs. Smith survived and, four years later, won the lawsuit.

As the years passed, Mrs. Smith became more passionate in her defense of Negro rights. Her newspaper in Jackson defended the Negro cause, condemned racial violence, and taunted the hooded segregationists. When cars with masked license plates begun to tail her, Mrs. Smith rushed up to one and tore off the tape hiding the license number. She reported it to the police, but to no avail.

In the summer of 1964, Mrs. Smith defended the civil rights workers and condemned the state for its violence. She advocated a military occupation if the state failed to change its ways. On August 28, whites retaliated by blowing up the offices of the *Northside Reporter* with a homemade bomb. Luckily, Mrs. Smith escaped injury. She carries on as before, writing searing editorials about injustice.

The writings of James Silver have also stirred Mississippi wrath and similar attempts to "get" him have been made. As a distinguished professor of history at "Ole Miss," Silver has served his state for close to thirty years. He has built up library collections, acted as chairman of his department (which under his tenure ranked among the South's best), and authored several histories of Mississippi. In 1962, he watched with dismay as the insurrection developed at his university over the admittance of James Meredith. As an individual, Silver did all he could to calm the rioters. He talked to students, patrolled the campus at night with other professors, and made small gestures of friendship to the Negro student. His house was stoned during the night of the riot, but a rush by federal soldiers saved it from severe damage. Silver led a group of professors who tried to correct the distortions put out by Mississippi newspapers about the university crisis ("University Invaded by Brutal Paratroopers Killing Two Co-eds") by publishing accurate descriptions of the situation. At his inauguration as president of the Southern Historical Association, Silver leveled devastating charges at Mississippi, calling the state a totalitarian society. "Given the great silence from the men of good will," he said, "and the disposition of the good people to let things run their course, there can be little hope for anything constructive in Mississippi in the next few years." [28]

In an effort to reverse the flow of public opinion, Silver wrote his eloquent *Mississippi: The Closed Society* in 1964. The book described the way in which Mississippi had become a society of the "closed mind" and had borne the eventual fruits of its system in the Oxford crisis. As Silver knew from his own experience, "When people are told from every public rostrum in the state on every day of their lives—and such is the case with the undergraduates who assaulted the marshals—that no authority on earth can legally or morally require any change in the traditional terms of Mississippi social life, this very process generates conditions that will explode into riot and insurrection." [29]

While Silver had written his book for Mississippians, the bookstores and newsstands in the state boycotted it. One could get a smuggled copy only surreptitiously. Nonetheless, word circulated about Silver's judicious, measured discussion of the state's problems. Several hundred Mississippians wrote him, most of them commending his bravery and judgment.

Silver suffered for his nonconformity. Former friends deserted him, newspapers bayed after him, and the university's board of regents informed him that he would be fired as soon as the board could find a way. (Since he had tenure at the university, a brazen dismissal might have caused the university to lose its accreditation once and for all.)

When I met him in July of 1964, Silver looked tired and sad. A tall, dark man with a deeply-lined face, he had just returned from several appearances before the press and television in the North. While berated in his own state, he had become a national figure, hounded by reporters in the rest of the country. A huge police dog accompanied him wherever he went in Oxford. Although Silver deprecated the dog's prowess ("He just slept soundly on the night of the riot"), the dog offered Silver some protection from marauders.

In talking about his role in the state, Silver refused to take credit for his individualism. "In no sense am I an activist," he said, "I avoid petitions and public stands as much as I can. It takes a lot more bravery for a Negro to put you up in his house than it does for me to write a book." Silver hoped that his work might pry open some closed minds. "I want to try to maintain some influence in the white community," he said, but then he added a little wistfully: "Sometimes, I'm sorry I am not on the battle line like Bob Moses, risking my life."

Silver's relation to the University of Mississippi was rather delicate. Many of his best friends had left the university or had retired. A few, such as an art instructor who had "desecrated the Confederate flag" by painting what he saw during the Oxford riots, had simply been dismissed. "Hell, I like it here," Silver commented about Oxford, "but I don't know how long I can stay. As far as I can see, the university will be entrenched in mediocrity for the next decade." In a recent exchange, the board of regents had called Silver in to explain why he had described Aaron Henry as the greatest man in Mississippi. "I tried to tell them of my respect for Henry's bravery. He is, after all, the man most likely to receive the Medgar Evers treatment, but he keeps on fighting. The regents just could not understand why I could tell reporters of my sympathy for a Negro."

Silver did not believe that progressive elements in Mississippi could do a great deal to change the state: "COFO's work is excellent. Every Negro child those workers teach can, of course, be considered as a mark of progress. But COFO can't bring about big changes because an organization like that cannot alter white public opinion. As for the Negroes in the state, they have been trained to be inferior, and they *are* inferior. The majority are scared and apathetic; around Oxford there are no obstacles to Negro voting, but still most Negroes stay away from the polls."

In Silver's view, the large moderate section among whites, particularly businessmen, could effect a revolution. But this seemed only a theoretical possibility. "I don't hold to very much hope about the businessmen. The White Citizens' Councils can strangle them with a boycott unless a majority of the more important men acted in unison. They are too scared to do that. Take an example: There are two druggists in this town. One of them would be happy to integrate his lunch counter. Instead, he has taken out the stools and closed it up. He knows that if he didn't, all of his business would go to the other store."

While Silver believed that "the end of segregation is inevitable," he saw its demise as taking a long time. He seemed to have lost hope that any significant group within the state could measurably change the pace of progress. His own future seemed equally in doubt. He was about to leave for a temporary appointment at Notre Dame. "I need to get away for a while," he said, expressing the fatigue which overcomes all white radicals in the state from time to time. "I don't know whether I'll return. In this atmosphere, I just live from month to month. There is no point in planning further."

Silver's pessimism about the immediate future was not shared by the Reverend Edwin King, perhaps the most active political leader in the ranks of white radicals. King believes that Mississippi Negroes can wield sufficient power to alter their subservient position. He has devoted all of his considerable energy to inspiring the Negro community and organizing it for political action.

King serves as chaplain and dean of students at Tougaloo College, a small but superior private school. The Negro college has a few white students and is the only truly integrated educational institution in Mississippi. Under the leadership of King and an excellent faculty, the school has pioneered in giving accelerated courses to prepare bright Negro students for college work. It has also become a center of civil rights agitation. Inevitably, the college has been the victim of segregationist ire. In the spring of 1964, the state legislature made plans to withdraw the school's accreditation and to disqualify Tougaloo graduates as teachers in the state.

In the eyes of segregationists, King has become the symbol of subversive agitation. His pedigree as a native Southerner did not save him from being dismissed from his first church or protect him from violence. Several years ago, unidentified whites pushed King's car off a country road. King survived the crash, but his body and face still bear the scars of the attack. Police have kept up the pressure on King. Now his gray Rambler has become so well known that he can hardly leave the Tougaloo campus without receiving a ticket.

He has not, however, allowed his fellow whites to force him out of the civil rights movement. In 1963, he ran for lieutenant governor on the Freedom Democratic party ticket. He campaigned in every hamlet in the state and, together with Aaron Henry, gained 82,000 votes. During the summer of 1964, he took on some of the hardest jobs in the civil rights movement. King was, for example, one of the first people to go to the Southwest to open the area for other workers who followed. He was also influential in organizing the Freedom Democrats. His work was recognized by the offer of a seat as a delegate-at-large to the national convention, a reward which he felt compelled to reject. At great personal risk, King has taken the lead in forging a potentially influential party, representative of Negro aspirations. He, along with two others—Episcopalian minister Duncan Cray and Monsignor Chatham of the Catholic church—symbolizes the active role which Christians might play in Mississippi.

The white radicals like King represent one side of the opposing forces at work in Mississippi. Quixotically heroic, they fight on without a real hope of victory. In the summer of 1964, people of this sort openly allied themselves with the Negro movement. Perhaps for the first time, they began to see some tangible results from their efforts. Although a tiny minority within the state, they gave a sure indication that the Mississippi mind had not completely degenerated into barbarism.

"The Inevitable Transition"

Reasonable Mississippians have repeatedly warned their fellow citizens that they cannot cling to their old myths and forever maintain a tyranny upon Negroes. "The only option Mississippians have," James Silver has written, "is whether to make an inevitable transition peaceable or bloody." [30] Even William Faulkner, often taken as a segregationist, spoke out at the end of his life in a solemn message to other whites: "We speak now against the day when our southern people who will resist to the last these inevitable changes in social relations, will, when they have been forced to accept what they at one time might have accepted with dignity and goodwill, say, 'Why didn't someone tell us this before?' 'Tell us this in time?' " [31]

Powerful forces work against these changes: organized bigots such as the White Citizens' Councils, years of indoctrination from every intellectual source, and the lethargy of custom. Sheer poverty and ignorance are perhaps the most effective brakes on change. White personal income in the state averages $1,200, about 50 per cent of the national level. More than 50 per cent of adult whites have only a grade-school education. In such an environment, one can hardly expect whites themselves to initiate a revolution in their social customs. Mississippi has been a closed society for so long that the moderate whites have felt, until recently, that the only alternative to their conformity would be persecution or exile. For those of the segregationist temper, the myths of racial superiority have given comfort and assurance. Abandoning these myths hurts, and it seems most unlikely that the backward and impoverished white majority will make the sacrifice voluntarily.

The nature of the Mississippi mind led most observers in 1964 to conclude that widespread violence would accompany social change in the state and that only a massive show of federal force would control white passions. In discussing the future of civil rights in Mississippi, social commentator Louis Lomax, for one, predicted that the whites would soon resort to violence. "Personally, I am convinced that only martial law can bring about token integration in these areas. The cost of providing Negroes with the unhampered and unpunishable right to vote will be high indeed, and the desegregation of public facilities in these areas will bring on such raw ugliness that we all will be forced to stop and ponder whether we are fighting a battle that can end only in a Pyrrhic victory." [32]

Yet, despite the deaths and bombings, thousands of Negroes *have* gained the vote, public facilities *have* been at least partially desegregated, and school integration *has* taken place. These gains occurred for a multitude of reasons. The Negroes' increasing unity scared the extremist whites; the presence of federal officers deterred white violence; the threat of lawsuits, revulsion in at least a part of the population against lawlessness, fear on the part of business leaders about danger to the economy—all these factors moderated the white resistance to integration. And, too, it is probably fair to say, as Gunnar Myrdal originally pointed out, that many whites in the deepest part of their conscience cannot completely deny the justice of Negro demands.

The events of 1964 indicate that many whites will tolerate significant changes in their social order if it is made abundantly clear to them that they have no other recourse. The "inevitable transition," as James Silver has called it, is now very much under way. But what we now know is that it will come only when the repressed Negroes, backed with national law, assert all of their latent economic and political power. Now that they are impressed with the majesty of their cause, Mississippi's Negroes will not wait much longer.

6

The Quiet Revolt:
Mississippi Negroes

AMBITIOUS Southerners, attracted by the promise of rich loam land, began to move into Mississippi around 1815. Along with their cattle and farm equipment, they imported a line of slaves. Sent overland through Tennessee or shipped from New Orleans, the slaves entered Mississippi territory in handcuffs and chains. Because of the great demand, slave breeders carried out experiments to increase the number of salable Negroes. By the age of twenty, many Negro women had already given birth to five children. These people—torn from their native cultures, deliberately separated from their families, and herded like animals—were the ancestors of the one million Negroes who now live in Mississippi.

During a brief respite after the Civil War, Mississippi Negroes escaped from slavery. Assisted by the Freedmen's Bureau, they secured fair wages for their work, established a system of free education, and participated in politics. For a time, they could ex-

pect equal treatment before the state's courts. Outnumbering the
whites by 100,000, they even succeeded in sending two Negro
senators to Washington.

The federal government did not, however, implement the sug-
gestions of the more radical reconstructionists. Negroes did not
receive either the training or enough land to make them economically self-sufficient. They had little choice but to return to
their old masters. And, during moments of crisis, the Negroes
could seldom mobilize the weaponry commanded by whites. Their
prime defense was federal power, and when this was gradually
withdrawn as a result of southern influence in Congress, the Negroes were left with few resources.

Between 1870 and 1900 the white man ruthlessly created a new
caste system to replace slavery. As the North turned its attention
away from Negroes, southern whites set about disfranchising them.
In the election of 1875, armed bands of whites roamed the state,
killing and mutilating Negroes at will. The election marked a
brutal end to Reconstruction policies in Mississippi and to the
state's Republican party. Under the new dispensation, the Negro
was again forced into economic servitude or, even worse, into a
convict-leasing system by which plantation owners "rented" prisoners from the state. The number of voting Negroes dropped
steadily: in 1867, 67,000 Negroes had registered to vote; by 1892,
only 8,000 remained on the rolls, and by 1900, only 2,000 could
vote. Negroes who opposed the resurrection of the conditions of
slavery were burned at the stake, hung, or run out of the state.

For the first fifty years of the twentieth century, the Negro was
subject to a relentless pressure to keep him inferior. He was not
allowed to vote, to hold even minor offices, or to attend decent
schools. He could not expect equal treatment in the courts or at his
work. He could not sit in the same churches with whites, go to the
same hospitals, or even at his death, lie in the same cemetery.
Between 1882 and 1963, 539 Negroes, more than in any other
state, were lynched in Mississippi. Bereft of economic or political

power and terrorized by lynching, the Negro had no other choice except to "keep in his place."

The great majority of Mississippi Negroes even today live out their existence in rural servitude. About 70 per cent attempt to earn their living from the land. Many are sharecroppers, obliged to buy and sell from a white plantation owner. Most of the remainder are seasonal workers who find work sporadically as cotton pickers or fruit harvesters. In classical Marxist form, they make up a pool of surplus labor which the white employer buys and sells at prices largely determined by him.

The rural cotton economy, on which Mississippi still depends, was built on the backs of Negroes. Those caught in its credit system have little chance to escape. Each year, the tenant farmer must buy his seeds and equipment from the plantation owner. The owner advances these supplies on account and, as the year progresses, deducts capital and interest from the Negro's produce. On many farms, the Negro must buy his sugar, coffee, and beans with company scrip at a company store. By the end of the year, he is left with a pitifully small amount of cash.

"I tell you a little how it is over there," one Negro described his conditions in the Delta. "They all live on somebody's big plantation, never know how much they are getting, go down to the store, 'Give me some flour, a sack of sugar, give me some Cokes,' go down get their clothes. End of the year comes, The Man [the white manager] hand him ten dollars, fifteen dollars, that's it. He don't even know. If he try to ask Man about it, He talk him right down." [1]

Another Negro farmer, writing to the National Sharecroppers' Fund, told of his life: "I'm colored, also a sharecropper. We live on a white employer plantation. We have no food in the house at all, and we have been nearly starving all year mostly. We need winter clothing, what can we do? Last year we made twenty-three bales of cotton, clear only $300. This year nineteen bales of cotton.—Don't care how much we made, we never clear nothing much. We have to borrow against the next year crop to buy food and clothes. This is why we never have anything." [2]

Until 1954, as we have noted, this system of economic slavery was effectively buttressed by other forms of coercion. If a rural Negro child wanted an education, he attended a decrepit school, financed at best with one-fifth the sum devoted to white children. If a Negro farmer wanted to better his skills, white officials cut him off from federal assistance. (Negro tenant farmers have received only 5 per cent of the farm improvement funds due to them, and recently the state killed a tractor training program, because 1,500 Negroes would have benefited from it.) And, of course, if a Negro tried to vote or basically to challenge the system in other ways, he lost his job, his home, his health, or his life.

As even a cursory knowledge of sociology would lead one to guess, these conditions of oppression were reflected in various social characteristics of the Mississippi Negro. During the 1950's one out of every three Negro marriages ended in separation. Usually, following the pattern first laid down by conscious policy during the slavery period, the mother was left in charge of her family. One out of five Negro births was illegitimate—a reflection, perhaps, of the slave traders' breeding program. Three times as many Negroes as whites had to seek relief and old-age pensions. And the Negro crime rate, at least as tabulated by white police, greatly exceeded that of whites.

Only one institution, the Negro Baptist church, served to integrate this disorganized community. Furnishing hope of salvation in the after-life—and friendship, financial aid, entertainment, dignity in this life—the church became the center of the Negro world. By avoiding controversy, the church earned the permission to function from the white masters.*

This, then, was the Negro community at mid-century: an im-

* In at least three instances during the summer of 1964, whites gave money to Negroes to help them rebuild their churches after a bombing attack. Significantly, the whites as a group never stepped forward to rebuild the homes of individual Negroes which had suffered attacks.

poverished, downtrodden group of peasants lacking legal, economic, and political power; a matriarchal society whose members found their solace in religion, sex, or crime; a servile class of serfs jumping obediently and smilingly to the orders of white masters. Except for the unchartered, expensive escape routes to New Orleans and Memphis—and from there to Detroit, Chicago, or New York—it was a world of no exit for the Negro. For the white man, it was a comfortable society, threatened only occasionally by dark rumblings from the world of Negro servants.

Almost imperceptibly, however, cracks appeared in this monolith. Mississippi's dependence on cotton declined from the 1930's on, and with it, the need for rural Negro labor. White farmers turned more to rice, cattle, soybeans, and increasingly, to mechanized production. Negroes migrated from the rural areas to Mississippi towns or to the North. In these new environments, they absorbed an ethic of freedom which could hardly be reconciled with what they had originally been taught.

Other forces were at work: Negro education improved slightly but steadily; the coming of radio and, eventually, television opened new vistas; intruders from the North—labor organizers and NAACP leaders—made cautious forays into the state to organize pockets of resistance against the white system. And, of course, many Mississippi men went abroad to fight for their country. Leaders like Medgar Evers, Aaron Henry, and James Meredith discovered in the armed forces a new sense of personal dignity, a new atmosphere of liberty. They returned to their state determined to play roles other than "Sambo" and "Rastus."

A quiet revolt had begun, but the white Southerner was loath to recognize it. Convinced of his superiority, self-congratulatory about his generosity, arrogant about his knowledge of "niggers," the average white could not believe that his hegemony was threatened.

Two events—the Negroes' reaction to the Supreme Court decision and, a decade later, the Negroes' response to Medgar Evers's assassination—shook the white man's complacency and awakened a sense of danger.

In 1954, hoping to stall action on the Supreme Court decision, Governor Hugh White called together a meeting of one hundred Negro leaders. By some absurd miscalculation, the governor felt confident that the Negroes would endorse the continuance of segregation. Instead, to his dismay, even the most conservative Negroes argued for abolition of the system. In vain, Governor White talked in generalities about the "happy race relations" of the past. His hopes that the Negroes would rubber-stamp the old system disappeared when the Reverend H. H. Hume, a known conservative, took the floor: "Gentlemen, you all should not be mad at us. Those were nine *white* men that rendered that decision. Not one colored man had anything to do with it. The real trouble is that you have given us schools too long in which we could study the earth through the floor and the stars through the roof." [3] Governor White exclaimed that "you couldn't trust the Negroes any more," and dismissed the conference in disgust.

For the more perceptive white men, the governor's conference marked the end of their illusions about Negroes. Leaders of the White Citizens' Councils, despite their public pronouncements, realized that they faced a fight. "We saw that Northern agitators had gotten to our Nigras," one segregationist told me. "We had to adopt new tactics."

The next decade, as we have remarked, was one of sporadic battles. A minority of Negroes launched school desegregation suits, attempted to win the vote, and sought to organize their fellow citizens into effective pressure groups. Two features of the Negro strategy during this period deserve attention: First, the battle was carried on by only a handful of leaders who, one by one, were decimated by white attacks. Second, the Negro leaders followed a path of gradualism. They believed that they might gain redress for their grievances in a peaceful, compromising fashion. Indeed, public opinion polls in 1962 showed that about 40 per cent of Negroes still believed that significant advances might be achieved simply by whites and Negroes sitting down to talk. In fact, the decade of the 1950's did not produce a single significant Negro advance in Mississippi.

Continuous defeats caused a change in the climate of Negro opinion. More than any other single event, the response to the martyrdom of Medgar Evers in June, 1963, symbolized the transition. Evers's murder released an unprecedented wave of anger from the long frustrated Negroes.

The Negro leaders, responding to this surge of unexpected support, changed their tactics. Rather than depending entirely upon a legalistic approach, they turned increasingly to direct action programs. They used their new rank-and-file support to initiate economic boycotts, freedom days, street demonstrations, political rallies. These activities stirred the imagination of the average Negro, for they gave him an active personal role in the movement. While still peaceful and orderly in nature, the new program of the 1960's threatened the white tyranny more massively, immediately, and openly.

Although exact estimates are difficult, perhaps 25 per cent of Mississippi Negroes can today be considered as active, militant participants in the drive to reform the state. Often drawn from the ranks of younger, urban people, it is this group which has joined the Freedom Democratic party, marched on picket lines, led boycotts, and risked jail sentences. And it is its wisdom and strength of will which will determine in large part the future course of Mississippi's revolt. I propose that we examine the attitudes of three of these militant Negroes—Evers, the renowned leader, and a boy and a girl who follow in his path—since these people, in the judgment of most observers, represent the Negroes of the future.

The Militant Negroes

Medgar Evers, a man who risked and lost all in his battle to change the Negro's place, has become the prototype of the "new"

Negro. His origins were unexceptional and gave little indication that he would become the hero of an entire generation of young Mississippi Negroes. Born of poor parents in Decatur, Evers learned early in life where he stood in the social and economic scale. He had grown up with a white playmate who lived next door to him. "Then, one day, my friend stopped coming by," Evers recalled in a 1960 interview. "In a little while, he began to get nasty. Finally, out in the street with a group of his friends, he called me 'nigger.' I guess at that moment I realized my status in Mississippi. I have lived with it ever since." [4]

Like thousands of other Mississippians, Evers joined the army and served in France and Belgium. There he learned of the African nationalist movement and the Mau Maus. In his despair, he dreamed for a time of leading Mississippi Negroes in a similar guerrilla campaign. As he matured, however, he realized that he "couldn't hate the white man and at the same time hope to convert him." (Nonetheless, although he had abandoned the methods of African nationalists, he named his first son Kenyatta.)

When he returned to his home state, Evers resolved that he would become a voting citizen. In his steamy little sawmill town of Decatur, nine hundred white men had registered, but not one Negro. In 1946, Evers went with his brother Charles and four other men to register at the clerk's office. Every night after that, groups of whites visited his parents and told them that their sons must withdraw their names. The day before an election, Senator Bilbo came to the town and told whites that the "best way to keep a nigger from the polls on election day is to visit him the night before." Nevertheless, on election day, the six Negro men gathered at Evers's home and walked to the polls. "I'll never forget it," Evers once said, "not a Negro was on the streets, and when we got to the courthouse, the clerk said he wanted to talk with us. When we got into his office, some fifteen or twenty armed white men surged in behind us, men I had grown up with, had played with. We split up and went home. . . . Well, in way we were whipped, I guess, but I made up my mind then that it would not be like that again—at least not for me." [5]

Evers went on to Alcorn College (a state Negro school, where students rioted in the spring of 1964 against segregation). He became a salesman for a local insurance company and, for some years, seemed to have accepted his lot as a dispossessed citizen. Yet, on his own, he reorganized several chapters of the NAACP. He revived one nearly dead branch of the organization in Cleveland, and soon had drawn five hundred members to it.

In 1954, Evers applied to the University of Mississippi Law School for admittance. Attorney General (later Governor) James P. Coleman called him to his office for an interview. Coleman plied him with questions, including a query about where he would stay if admitted to the university. "On the campus, sir," Evers told him, "I'm very hygienic. I bathe every day, and I assure you this brown won't rub off." [6] Evers received notice several days later that his application had been refused because he did not have the proper recommendations.

In December of that year, he became full-time member of the NAACP field staff. One of the reasons he joined, Evers later recalled, was because of the circumstances which had surrounded his father's death. When his father was suffering from internal bleeding, he was rushed to a Negro hospital. By chance, another Negro who had been in a fight with police was also brought into the emergency ward. A mob of whites came searching for the man, peering in the window, yelling for the skin of the "nigger." "My dad died a short time later," Evers remembered, "and outside, these whites were demonstrating like animals. . . . A Negro cannot live here or die here in peace as long as things remain the same." [7]

Having become the NAACP leader for the state, Evers roamed from town to town, cajoling Negroes into active participation. He sponsored lawsuits (one including his own children) to enforce the Supreme Court decision, and he organized an NAACP youth corps. Just before he was killed, he had secured some 10,000 members for the state NAACP.

Evers achieved much of his success with the "little men"—farmers and laborers—who, hired by whites at minor tasks, could have easily lost their jobs by joining the NAACP. Evers's phenomenal memory for names, his own rural background, and his willingness to travel to every part of the state (he would log 78,000 miles a year in recruiting drives) overcame the natural hesitance of this group to participate in the civil rights fight.

He also concentrated on organizing young people who had not yet been indoctrinated into the posture of servility. One friend recalls seeing Evers in a Jackson restaurant when two children approached him. One little boy pulled out an NAACP membership card. "There it is Mr. Evers," the boy said, smiling widely, "my card finally came." "Aw shucks," another boy responded, "That's nothing, I've been an NAACP member for a long time." Evers confessed to his friend that organizing the young people, while necessary in providing future leadership, was an unpleasant task. "That's what I mean about this race business . . . at their ages most white boys don't have to be concerned with anything more serious than where to play tomorrow, or some childhood foolishness like the secret signs and passwords of their television heroes." [8] But for Negro children, Evers believed, the commitment to serve their community had to come early in life.

As Evers gained increasing success as a leader of Negroes, the whites started a vendetta against him. In Meridian, as he sat in a bus waiting to begin one of his many tours of the state, police grabbed him for sitting in one of the front seats. After being threatened by the police, he returned to the bus, again sitting toward the front. Just after the bus started up again, a white taxicab driver pulled in front of it, jumped in, and slugged Evers in the face. He took it calmly: "You can't let your emotions run away with you. If I had retaliated, it would have helped defeat the cause for which I am struggling."

By 1955, whites had publicized his name as one of nine men who had to be killed. The list quickly dwindled: The Reverend George Lee was shot to death in his home. Gus Courts left the state after he was wounded by a gunshot blast. Dr. R. M. Howard went to Chicago after repeated threats on his life, and Dr. Clinton Battle left for North Carolina after his home was bombed.

Medgar Evers knew the risk that he was taking and he faced it consciously and valiantly. "You just don't have time to be afraid," he said after Lee had been killed. Evers decided to stay in Mississippi despite the danger. "I'll be damned," he said in 1960, "if I'm going to let the white man lick me. There's something out here that I've got to do for my kids, and I'm not going to stop until I've done it." [9]

In June of 1963, at the height of his powers, when he had assured his leadership of the Negro movement and recruited thousands to the cause, Evers was felled by a shot in the back. His death did not end his influence in Mississippi: Negroes marched in the streets, founded a memorial fund in his name, and decorated their homes with pictures of this brave, determined man. More people attended his funeral than that of any other man in recent Mississippi history. Parents named newborn children after him, and young people vowed their allegiance to him in religious ceremonies.

While Medgar Evers was an exceptional leader of the new militant Negro, there are many others in Mississippi who are following his example. The core of support comes from young activists, most of whom are relatively well educated. Because of disappointment in the ways of "gradualism," they are alienated from the traditional Negro leadership in the state. They look upon the Negro professional class as "Uncle Toms" and often regard the Negro church with disdain. Having witnessed a decade of apparently futile legal battles, they are eager to try more direct means of changing their station in life. They are tough, even reckless, and quite willing to go to jail for their cause. Indeed, a jail sentence has become an indispensable badge of merit to many Negro high-school and college students.

A typical representative of the "left wing" of these young activists is "James McLain," * a lean, hardened young leader from southwest Mississippi. McLain was raised on a farm by his widowed mother. When times were hard, he was sent to live with an uncle in Jackson. There he was carefully instructed in the customs of servitude: he had to call every white man "sir," he could not even glance at a white woman, and he had to accept without question whatever wages were offered him for his work.

At the age of fifteen, he traveled around the state looking for jobs. It was during these lonely journeys that McLain ran into experiences of discrimination which he never forgot. In one town, for example, he got off the bus and looked around in vain for other Negroes. Since he had to sleep somewhere for the night, he approached a white man and told him politely that he was a stranger. "Sir," he asked, "can you please tell me where Negroes hang around in this town." "Over there," the white man said, laughing uproariously as he pointed to a tree in the middle of the town square. Memories such as these rankled in McLain's mind and gradually created in him a fanatic hatred of white men.

McLain finished high school in Jackson and then enlisted to fight in the Korean war. He returned to Jackson but failed to find any work. "For several years, I was little more than a gangster," he told me. "I hung around street corners, did odd jobs and even ran a little dope. I was bitter as a man can be. I learned to kill during the war, and more than anything else, I wanted to kill a white man. If one ever came near me, I reached instinctively for my pocket knife."

In 1961, he attended by chance a street rally where Robert Moses spoke. Moses exhorted the audience to fight for their rights by going to the polls. "That meeting with Moses was the turning

* For obvious reasons, a fictitious name.

point in my life," McLain remembered. "He gave me hope and a chance to fight for better things. Without his influence I might still be on the streets. If you have no other channel for your anger, it will spill out in knife fights or sluggings."

Moses put McLain to work in the freedom movement. He tackled some of the most difficult jobs. In 1962, he went into Rankin County to organize voters. His headquarters were bombed several times, and he was forced to sleep in a different home each night. He talked sixty men into registering to vote, signed up NAACP members, and encouraged some families to file desegregation suits against the school system. But McLain faced discouraging obstacles in his work. The sheriff of Rankin County told him that if "a nigger ever got in his jail, he would never come out alive." Support in the Negro community dwindled when paychecks and relief envelopes carried warnings that any Negro who registered to vote would lose his income. Nevertheless, McLain eventually succeeded in organizing a permanent citizenship club whose members tried to win the vote.

In 1964, McLain moved on to the quieter atmosphere of Vicksburg where he helped to equip a freedom school. Built on the crest of a hill, the school was impregnable to the attacks which anonymous whites repeatedly threatened. Perhaps because of its tourist orientation, Vicksburg offered relatively little resistance to the COFO invasion. When McLain escorted sixty potential voters to the registrar's office, forty succeeded in getting the vote.

In July of 1964, McLain was one of the seven men chosen to initiate operations in the Southwest. Three of us—McLain, another white and I—drove south to deliver him to his assignment. McLain picked out a circuitous route to follow, since he had been briefed on the danger spots along the way. The rented car carried Rankin County plates to avoid identification. As dusk approached, we entered a backroad, hilly area near McComb, and after exchanging signals with guards, reached an isolated farmhouse. From this headquarters, McLain was to organize political activity in a previously dormant area.

After shades had been drawn and kerosene lamps lit, McLain rested, surrounded by a group of Negro farmers. They were in an uneasy mood. A neighborhood church had been bombed the previous night and Schwerner, Chaney, and Goodman had disappeared only two weeks before. The farmers had guns with them, ready for use.

"I get to hating, too," McLain told them, trying to dampen the spirit of violence, "but it just takes too much of you to hate all the time. I used to carry a knife, and all I thought of was cutting a white man. But now, I've been fighting for three years, doing constructive things. I just don't have the energy to hate anymore. We have more important things to do."

He got the farmers to singing his favorite songs: "Striving for Freedom," "I'm Going To Turn on the Light of Freedom," "We Shall Overcome." Clapping and smiling, the farmers lost some of their bitterness. Before the evening was over, McLain had set plans for a voters' rally and lined up precinct captains to organize the district. "It's good to be with human beings again," he told them as the farmers slipped off one by one to their homes.

When, at 4 A.M., we finally went to bed, McLain was exhausted (two of the farmers, we later found, slept on the floor to provide us with beds). "I get as angry as they do," McLain said, just before sleeping. "I could have killed Beckwith after they let him off for shooting Evers. And when I got word about Philadelphia—Mike Schwerner was a good friend of mine—a bunch of us almost drove there to shoot up the town. But somehow, we have to keep all this hatred under control. I don't know how long we can do it."

Like so many of the young activists, McLain could not believe that the future held out much hope for him. "I'd like to go on to college. I'd like to forget my skin for a while. I'd even like to look at a white girl without thinking of the rope that would be waiting for me. But probably I'll end up like Mike did, or maybe they will just cart me off to New Orleans." (The city had become a rest stop for civil rights workers who broke under strain.)

At eight the next morning, McLain had already left the farm for a tour of the neighborhood. He worked demoniacally and, by summer, he had established a permanent freedom school in the area and encouraged several hundred people to become voters.

Young people like McLain will furnish the professional leadership for Negroes in the future. They are bitter, ready to take risks and, on the whole, willing to use nonviolent techniques *only* as long as this strategy wins a response from white consciences. They shun publicity and look down upon the current crop of national Negro leaders. (McLain referred to Martin Luther King as "De Lawd" because of King's alleged tendency to seek the limelight.) Their determination has a grim and rather frightening quality about it. Unlike their predecessors—the Negro ministers and teachers who sought to accommodate themselves to the white man's world—these new leaders will not allow the whites to rest.

In the ranks of Mississippi activists (at least for the present) McLain can be considered as a "firebrand," a bit to the left of the mainstream. "Sandra Craig," a Jackson State College student, is perhaps more typical of the new generation of militant Negroes. A slender, beautiful girl of eighteen, "Sandy" is not unaware of her charms. She is proud of her male conquests, pleased with the milk chocolate color of her skin, and addicted to fashion magazines. She has done some modeling and seems more concerned with dating the captain of the basketball team than with the Negro revolt.

She has not entirely cut herself off from the pathetic tendency of Mississippi Negroes to imitate the white world; her bedroom wall displays a picture of herself decked out as a southern belle, making her debut at a society ball. Like all American teen-agers, Sandy recites her extracurricular activities as badges of acceptance: she edited her college paper, worked on the yearbook, and was voted "the most versatile girl" in her class.

Yet Sandy is not just a pretty paper doll, a Negro version of the usual vapid co-ed. I learned about the other side of Sandy's character when we met at a restaurant where she worked as a waitress near the COFO headquarters in Jackson. (She made three dollars a night from 6 to 12, earning money for college.)

Sandy plans to become a lawyer. "I'm tired of seeing my people cheated by second-class lawyers who really don't do anything for them," she said. "I want to help them." Sandy's plan for the future may not mature, but in the meantime she has already done a great deal for the Negro cause. When Medgar Evers lost his life, Sandy led her classmates in a protest march. "We were well dressed, clean, and from good families," she said, with a touch of pride in recalling the incident. "They put hundreds of us in jail for disturbing the peace. . . . But it was lots of fun. All of the young kids sang, some prayed. We kept those cops up all night." The students were released, but they kept demonstrating in Jackson throughout the summer of 1963. The police jailed the youngsters repeatedly, usually charging them with parading without a permit. In August, for some reason, the arrests stopped.

Sandy turned to voter registration work. At first she escorted her parents (the owners of a dry-cleaning establishment) to the city hall. "They passed the first time, but then the registrar got hard. We had to take people back two or three times. Eventually they passed. It seemed so easy, until we learned that they had changed the poll tax rules. You can't vote now unless you have paid the tax two years in a row. That can stymie us. Two years from now, they will think up some new rule to stop people from voting."

During the summer of 1964, Sandy came to COFO headquarters looking for work. She was sent out as a messenger and distributor of freedom registration ballots. She enjoyed the excitement around COFO headquarters and her first social contacts with white teenagers.

One night, perhaps unwisely, she gave a party at her home. Both white and Negro youngsters came, dancing barefooted on the lawn. While perfectly decorous under other conditions, the party created fear in Sandy's neighbors who watched the strange phenomenon from behind their window shades. The next night, two carloads of white men cruised up and down the dirt road in front of her home. They abstained from attacking, but their presence was enough to earn Sandy a reprimand from her parents.

On another day during the summer, Sandy walked gaily into the COFO office and asked: "Who wants to get a Coke with me at the dime store?" Two other girls responded excitedly that they would accompany her. As they left, four photographers from national magazines followed them. At first, I could not understand the commotion. Then, of course, it dawned on me that this would be a test of the Civil Rights Law, one more of those unplanned, slightly reckless ventures which eventually proved the law's validity in Jackson. The store served the girls a Coke—and threw out the photographers.

Sandy also began going to Jackson's white library. Facilities for Negroes are inadequate and, until recently, Negroes did not dare to read books at the white library. Sandy, with some other young people, challenged this rule. Police have followed her after each of her library visits and have demanded the driver's license of whoever drove her. While she has been met with glacial reserve, Sandy has broken down one more of Mississippi's barriers to Negro advance.

Sandy is no heroine. She is a somewhat frivolous, pleasantly naïve girl, who happens to be in a generation which finds civil rights work as normal as joining a sorority. She recognizes that her age group represents a distinct change from the past. "We're different. I take one look at the president of my college and I can see that. A few months ago, Mayor Thompson got this man up before TV with him. Thompson praised the president to the skies. He talked about what a good man he was, how Jackson was the closest thing to heaven on earth, and how Negroes were so well treated. You know what this Jackson State man did? He just nodded, and smiled, and said, 'Yes suh.' " Sandy purposively put on a southern Negro drawl. "That type is going fast. No more of that cottoning-up for us!"

Another way that Sandy—and a significant part of her generation—has changed has been her rejection of traditional Protestanism. In her case, Sandy became attracted to Catholicism. "I like the ceremony, the feeling it gives you of really being in church, and the way they act instead of talk." For one year, she attended a parochial school ("Sister told us that it would be integrated soon, but that this year might be a little dangerous"). Many of the young activists have either abandoned their religion totally or turned to a new one. The Black Muslim movement has made no inroads in Mississippi—indeed, Negroes just laughed at Malcolm X's offer to provide guerrilla warriors in the state—but the same motives that impel northern Negroes to become Muslims have led younger southern Negroes to question their old religion. In both cases, the new generation has found that the balm of traditional religion no longer quiets their longings. Catholicism (as symbolized in the Jackson Cathedral's mosaic of whites and Negroes under one God) offers many of the activists like Sandy a new sense of brotherhood.

These young people, cut in the same mold as Sandra Craig, are carrying the freedom movement forward with a momentum that Mississippi never knew before. In a variety of small ways—taking their parents to vote, entering formerly forbidden white preserves, reading books in a library which had been denied them—these activists have ripped themselves away from the traditional Mississippi moorings.

What does Sandra Craig have in common with James McLain and Medgar Evers? There is, of course, the sense of unjustified humiliation, the sometimes spoken but usually hidden bitterness. But beyond these feelings—which must have characterized all American slaves—the Mississippi militants exhibit new qualities. They still value education (but do not think of it as race salvation); they regard the law as a useful ally (but certainly not as all-powerful); they will take the nonviolent path (but seldom from Gandhian convictions). They have lost many of the old faiths and now seem determined to mold a future through other means. Whether their new approach—politics, picketing, and parading—can win depends on swinging the majority of outwardly docile Negroes to their side. These quiet ones form the mass of Mississippi Negroes.

The "Submissive" Negroes

They cannot be described as contented, or servile, or even passive. Rather, the majority of Mississippi Negroes simply wait, quietly and with determination, for a propitious time to assert their demands. Their white masters—the ladies whom they serve as maids, the men for whom they work in the fields—haven't the slightest idea what goes on behind the resigned, cheerful faces presented to them. From long training, the Mississippian Negro has learned to put up an inscrutable façade to the white man and to flatter him into thinking that he can understand what emotions pass through the quiet Negro's mind. But even the apparently submissive Negroes, comprising some 75 per cent of the nonwhite population, have begun to stir fitfully from their slumber. They do not yet dare to imitate Medgar Evers nor even their own children. Yet, when they can take action without fear of immediate identification and retaliation, they do. The fact that tens of thousands of Negro adults have joined the Freedom Democratic party is one measure of the scope of their protest.

The submissive Negroes generally come from rural areas, particularly from the sprawling plantations where "The Man" still rules. They usually have little education (some 10 per cent of Mississippi Negroes are, in fact, illiterate) and no economic resources to use in times of emergency. They stem from an older age group which has lost many of its natural leaders to the northern emigration.

A typical representative of these people is "Bernice Miller," a women of fifty who lives on an isolated Mississippi farm. I became acquainted with Mrs. Miller and her family through a series of accidents which do not need to be recited here. My white skin was, of course, a barrier to confidence; but through working together for a long period of time, her fears and my inhibitions gradually disappeared. We came to the point where she called me "Villiam," gently mimicking my wife's Danish accent.

Mrs. Miller had experienced most of the humiliations of a rural Negro woman. Raised on a farm with five brothers and sisters, she had worked long hours in the field picking cotton. She went to a primary school, but her parents could not afford to support her through high school.

As a girl she had had to submit to the white man's rudeness. She resented for years being told to move to the back of the bus or to give up her seat for white men. (Perhaps her greatest moment of triumph came after the freedom rides when she refused to give her seat to a white man who demanded it.)

Sexual attacks from whites were common during her younger years. "They didn't want integration during the day," she remembered, "but they sure wanted it at night." Once, while riding in a wagon to a store, a white policeman stopped her. He said he would arrest her if she would not come with him into the bushes. When she refused and struggled with him, he took her off to jail. After a night there, her father rescued her. "He almost exploded, he was so mad. But what could he do? He just looked daggers at that cop."

Mrs. Miller married at eighteen, following the pattern of youthful matrimony common in Mississippi. She bore her husband three daughters before he deserted her. For the last ten years, she has been the sole provider for the family. Her income comes partially from her husband's army pension (he died several years after leaving her) and from the farm's produce. In good years she received $150 a month in cash. She must pay $60 of her monthly income for the mortgage on her house, and half of this sum is compounded interest. When she purchased the farm, her white landlord, following the usual practice in farming areas, did not find the time to explain to Mrs. Miller how much of her payments would actually go toward buying the house.

She has little money left to care for her family. Their normal diet consists of bread, beans, greens, and occasionally, salt pork. One of her grown-up daughters had migrated to New York. The remaining two attend high school and, hopefully, one of them may go on to college. Mrs. Miller has stocked her farm with books, including the complete works of Shakespeare which she found discarded in the garbage can at a white home where she worked as a maid. Her children have been raised with a respect for learning.

Mrs. Miller's life is hardly an enviable one: days in the field; nights spent resting, reading, or listening to spirituals on the radio; perpetual fear that the landlord might foreclose (if she missed one installment on the house, the contract would lapse); and always, the pressure of hiding her contempt and hatred for whites.

She, like every Mississippi Negro whom I learned to know well, had an ambivalent relation to whites, a mixture of hatred and pity, humorous condescension and fear. She laughed at the whites' amorous advances toward Negro women and took her own light skin as ample evidence of segregation's incompleteness. She could dismiss the orations of southern demagogues with a smile and scoff at their excuses for maintaining segregation. "The whites are afraid that we would take over," she said in explaining southern intransigence. "Look what we have done, even in the position they gave us. We have the brains; if the whites would only allow a free' open fight, we would wallop them."

The bitterness is never far below the surface. She often apologized, for example, because of the outward appearance of her farm. It was a ramshackle, unpainted structure, although inside she kept it immaculate and took pride in its few furnishings. "I'd like to clean it up on the outside, but as soon as a Negro does that and gets himself a nice-looking little cottage, the whites think he is getting uppity. And that can bring trouble down on you."

Her hatred of the white man became apparent one day when her daughter suffered arrest at a voters' rally. The daughter had gone into the local county seat to watch older Negroes line up for registration. Caught in the spell of the moment she had joined in some freedom chants, and the police had whipped the girl off to jail. Mrs. Miller received notice to appear before the local judge.

She did so with apprehension. Never before had she been involved, even indirectly, in civil rights activity. She had not registered to vote herself, had not joined the NAACP, and had never even attended meetings concerned with the issue of Negro rights. Going before the white judge to rescue her daughter both frightened and humiliated her.

At the police station, the judge lectured the assembled parents and asked them all to pledge that their children would not work for civil rights in the future. One Negro mother gave in to the demand. She took her son by the ear and led him away. The other children begged their parents not to demean themselves. In an unusual outburst of anger, Mrs. Miller responded to the judge: "You may say you are concerned about our children, you don't want them to be taken in by agitators. But why don't you give us some of our rights? Why do you use dogs on our children?" Mrs. Miller's daughter had to remain in jail several days more.

One night after her daughter had returned home, Mrs. Miller shyly produced a poem which she had composed when the girl had been imprisoned. It revealed a depth of antagonism which Mrs. Miller, like other quiet Negroes, normally keeps carefully under cover:

> For you see I am Mr. White Man
> And you're just a nigger.
> Every time you raise your hand
> I start pulling my trigger.

You ain't nothing in God's sight
And you ain't nothing in mine.
What I say is always right
And Nigger you better mind.

You see I got dogs every day
I got guns and I've got a stick.
If you don't do what I say
I'll get you quick.

I'll put my dogs on your babies
I'll not even have to pay.
When I speak I don't mean maybe.
You gonna do just what I say.

To me you ain't much as cattle
God made me superior to you.
Before I let you start a battle
I'll kill every one of you.

You couldn't find a better state,
So the white man says.
If this is best, God help the worst,
Is the prayer I prays.

Although Mrs. Miller hated the southern system, there was little that she felt could be done to change it. What progress occurred would come through supernatural forces. "God will look out for us Negroes; He just won't let the whites keep shoving us around." Mrs. Miller, like many of the apparently passive Negroes, was convinced that God actively advanced the Negro cause. "Every time those whites kill a Negro—like Till, like Parker, like Medgar Evers—God takes his revenge. For every Negro who dies, one hundred whites meet their death. Just after Till was killed, some trains crashed. A lot of whites died; that was no accident, that was God's revenge."

She believed in a religious ethic which had little in it of the nonviolence preached by Martin Luther King. For her, God was all-powerful and would forcefully protect His people. Like that of most Mississippi Negroes, her religion did not have much room for the gentler virtues which have been described as the unique contribution the Negro revolt will eventually make to American culture.

Mrs. Miller's world revolves around religion: she begins the day by listening to spirituals on a Negro radio station, ends it by reading the Bible, and devotes most of Wednesdays and Sundays to her Baptist activities. Her vacation consists of a few days spent at a Negro religious camp. She is fully aware of the defects in her church: "The preacher can't talk, the organist thinks she is a big shot, the sisters spend all their time gossiping, and the brothers cheat on supplies for church dinners." These human frailties do not, for some reason, diminish the church's glory for her. It has been a haven from the world's frustrations and, until very recently, both congregation and preacher have wished to stay as far away from civil rights conflicts as possible.

After the arrest of her daughter, Mrs. Miller and other members of her church tentatively essayed the possibilities of entering the struggle more actively. Mrs. Miller attended a precinct meeting of the Freedom Democratic party (held at her church) and suddenly found herself elected to the county committee. For good or ill, she is now, more or less inadvertently, the leader of civil rights work in her rural community. In her response to the summer of 1964, Mrs. Miller resembled many of the previously docile Negroes. A combination of circumstances, largely beyond their control have drawn them into a vortex of activity. Their suppressed grievances now have a channel of expression.

Some Mississippi Negroes, unlike Mrs. Miller have not even been peripherally engaged in the civil rights struggle. These Negroes completely avoided personal involvement in the events of 1964. They cannot be called "Uncle Toms," for such types hardly can be found any more.* Rather, they are outwardly apathetic

* Perhaps, at some points in southern history, a group of Negroes did feel allegiance to the whites and may even have been grateful about the more benign aspects of slavery and segregation. Today, there are possibly a thousand Negroes in the state who receive pay as informers or make public statements condemning civil rights activity. They are well identified in the community but don't fit the usual "Uncle Tom" stereotype. A study of their motives would be a fascinating excursion into individual psychopa-

people, so thoroughly cowed by white power that they dare not resist it, at least for the moment. A leader of this most conservative section of Negro opinion, "Reverend Richard Deakin," exhibits the prudence which governs this dwindling but still significant part of the Negro community.

I met Deakin only with difficulty and our conversations had to take place at night. As the leader of a large Baptist congregation in Jackson, Deakin felt he could not endanger his position or that of his church by any open contact with the civil rights movement. Once, a year ago, he had given a mild sermon on the obligation to vote. Later, he had invited a white preacher to lead several prayer meetings. The result of these apparently harmless actions was that arsonists set fire to his church and burned it to the ground. Although Deakin found empty kerosene tins scattered around the charred site, fire inspectors claimed that the conflagration had been an accident.

Not unexpectedly, he lost a large part of his congregation. The remaining members rebuilt the church using their own cash and labor. (Like many Negro churches, Deakin's had not carried insurance.) He feared, perhaps rightly, that his board might dismiss him if he again took even a mildly open stand against segregation. "I wish I could invite you to worship at my church," he told us, "but it is just too dangerous. The brothers and sisters wouldn't stand for it." He quickly added, "They would love to have white people in the meeting, but after the burning, they're just too scared." Teachers formed a significant part of his congregation and they were perhaps the most timid. They had been told that the price of "getting out of line" would be the loss of their jobs.

As a central figure among Jackson Negroes, Deakin had a full opportunity to observe discrimination in all of its variations. He talked chiefly, of course, about the major forms of oppression: Negroes could not walk the streets at night for fear that police

thology. They are undoubtedly driven by the same obscure forces that led some Jews to betray others in Nazi concentration camps.

would arrest them on suspicion; Negroes could not escape the credit system of Jackson stores which kept them in bondage to high interest rates; Negroes could not secure the same jobs as whites, regardless of their skill.

In some ways, however, the more symbolic types of white contempt for Negroes disturbed the minister more than the objective costs of segregation. "I remember our Mayor talking about how grand the city was and how important Negroes were to its life. Then came a big memorial parade—the only Negroes in it were two men who walked behind the horses, cleaning up after them." He noted, too, how housing segregation had appeared in Mississippi for the first time. Because traditional southern housing patterns had mixed whites and Negroes in the same area, Mississippi has never produced the ghetto pattern so prevalent in the North. (Even Simmons, the White Citizens' Councils leader, was living next door to a Negro family in 1964.) Recently, however, the city has erected green fences which separate previously integrated white and Negro areas. "These are tangible barriers marking our inferiority," Deakin remarked, "and we hate them because they stake us off so clearly."

For several nights in a secluded meeting place, we talked about the heavy burden of discrimination. Deakin, despite the apathetic demeanor he presented to the whites and to his own churchgoers, hated the whole system. Yet, his background and his present position militated against any positive action.

As a child, he had been raised in a sharecropping area of the Delta. "I had to walk three miles to my school. On the way, I passed two new white schools, until I reached our place. It used to make me mad to get the books that they handed down from the white kids. I wondered why we couldn't have nice books too." He had wanted to become a truck driver or a fireman. But in Mississippi he could not even fulfill these modest ambitions. "They just didn't allow Negroes to drive buses or even garbage trucks. Even today, the Negroes can't drive the garbage trucks. They only haul the stuff up and dump it in."

At eighteen, he received "the call" and went into the Baptist ministry. After he went through a cursory education at a local Negro seminary, he became a part-time minister. Eventually, his speaking ability and religious fervor won him a commanding place with religious Negroes in Jackson. After formerly having to work in the cotton fields to keep his parents alive, Deakin found his new eminence most enjoyable. He was naturally hesitant about relinquishing the privileges of his position: a 1954 Buick, decent clothes, respect from his congregation, a nice house. He did not want to risk his security in a possibly losing battle for civil rights.

He, like many Negroes, had chosen a path of acquiescence. Underneath, resentment against the white world boiled within him, but to express it required the courage of Medgar Evers. Deakin did not have the makings of a hero. When his church burned down, he lost the will to protest, although he admired those who carried on the fight. (His last words, as we parted, were, "I am so glad you are here. We all are. Without the whites from the North, we would be lost.")

The Passing of the Submissive Negro

In attempting to assess the present condition of Mississippi Negroes, I have thought it best to draw portraits of more or less typical individuals. The usual methods of social science reporting simply do not apply in a situation as volatile as that of Mississippi. Public opinion polls, for example, can hardly give an accurate picture of Negro attitudes, since the average person, particularly in rural areas, would be extremely cautious about revealing his opinions to a casual visitor. Thus, it is impossible to make generalizations about the Mississippi Negro with any degree of certainty. Nonetheless, from the diverse and rather intimate contacts I had with the Negro community throughout the state, I believe that certain tentative generalizations can be ventured:

1. The ranks of submissive Negroes are steadily being eroded. While many like the Reverend Deakin remain outwardly docile, there are a substantial number of other people, who, like Bernice Miller, are willing to assume new responsibilities. The growth of the Freedom Democratic party, the large-scale riots in McComb, the continuing boycott in Greenwood, indicate that the revolt in Mississippi has now become a truly mass movement.

Many forces push toward ending Negro docility: urbanization, the influence of mass media and education, and the knowledge that most of the nation will back up a Negro revolt with legal, moral, and perhaps material assistance.

2. White violence no longer serves to keep Negroes in a state of perpetual servitude. For a few people like Deakin, a church burning may succeed in keeping discontent from turning into action. For most Negroes, however, white terrorism seems increasingly to mobilize and unify the community. One can cite many recent events where white brutality has appeared to increase rather than stifle Negro resistance. Medgar Evers's death drew thousands of Negroes who had not been previously involved into the civil rights battle; the multiple bombings in McComb eventually brought forth a violent response from the town's Negroes; the mass jailing of young people, as in Jackson, inflamed formerly apathetic parents. After centuries of success, white terrorism is now not only failing to fulfill its goals but is actually a major force igniting the Negro revolt.

3. The younger generation shows every sign of increasing militance. For it, the instruments of direct action—picketing, sit-ins, parades—have the greatest appeal. Regardless of their immediate effectiveness, these means will be used increasingly during the coming years. Older people admire the courage of those who participate in demonstrations and, generally, seem to believe that direct clashes with the white power system serve to dramatize the Negro cause. Nevertheless, few older people—except for the *very*

old who feel they have nothing to lose—will personally take part in demonstrations.

4. In the immediate future, all those between twenty and sixty —the majority of Negroes—will use two weapons in their attempt to escape from bondage: economic action and political agitation. During the last year, Negroes in urban areas have found that the boycott is a most effective means of protest. In Jackson, discriminatory employers have suffered a boycott by almost 100 per cent of the Negro community; and in Greenwood, perhaps 40 per cent of the Negroes have engaged in boycotting against businessmen who have participated most actively in the repression of Negroes. The boycott has the advantage of mass effectiveness and relative anonymity.

Most Negroes also put great, perhaps inordinate, faith in the electoral process as a way of improving their situation. The drive for voter registration will continue, and assuming that the federal government ensures freedom of registration, a significant block of Negro voters will soon emerge in Mississippi. A straw ballot taken in November, 1964, indicated how Negroes would have voted if they had had the chance: 63,000 voted for Johnson; 17 for Goldwater. This new political power will be used to change the local situation: the most brutal sheriffs will lose their jobs; county officials will have to be more equal in their distribution of federal largesse; and state representatives will find less and less political profit in baiting the Negro.

5. The possibility that Negroes will turn to violence cannot be discounted. It must be kept in mind that a very large share of the Negro population—virtually 100 per cent of independent farmers —is armed. They have not used these weapons as yet, but in a mood of desperation they easily could. Negro leadership strongly discourages the thought of violence, but people still talk of it as a genuine alternative. In the Southwest, in the hill region, and in the Jackson slums, even minor incidents might trigger bloody riots. Any retrogression, any major attempt by the whites to reverse the

advances of 1964, could be the signal for armed revolt.

Whether the Negroes' majestic experiment in nonviolence ends in a general conflagration—and, of course, defeat for their cause —depends largely upon the response of America as a nation to Negro aspirations. Informed with moral vision, willing to enforce the law with determination, Americans can demonstrate once again the nation's capacity to create a more just, more equitable, more reasonable society. In Mississippi, we are faced with a social revolution. It cannot be stopped. The only real question is whether Mississippi Negroes will fight their battles in lonely, bitter isolation or, rather, in alliance with all of those forces in American life which seek to ensure a humane society for us all.

7

An End to the Beginning

THE day-and-night terror experienced by the Mississippi Negro is so foreign to most Americans that we have difficulty in understanding the feeling. I have tried in this book to describe the Negro's anguish and to portray the Mississippi dictatorship, as far as an outsider can. But can you, reading this narrative, know what it is really like to watch every passing policeman, aware that he could be your murderer? Can you feel the fear which comes when a strange car, its wheels crunching quietly and too slowly, moves toward you over a deserted road? Can you understand that feeling of seeing men in a voter registration line disappear one by one into a police van, knowing you will be next if you have the courage?

I doubt that the usual prose can convey what it is like. Intimidation, harassment, beatings, bombings, killings—somehow these words lose their force when one has to repeat them so often in describing human behavior. Perhaps the best way to convey the nightmarish reality experienced by Mississippi Negroes and civil rights workers is to recount in their own sworn words the indignities which they have suffered.

Several hundred of these first-person reports exist, since COFO was anxious to secure affidavits to be used as unimpeachable evidence of Mississippi's lawlessness. They tell in detail and in the simple, direct language of those who experienced it what it was like to live in Mississippi during the long, hot summer of 1964. Rabbi Arthur Leyveld has told of his beating in Hattiesburg; Silas McGhee (before his face was smashed by a shotgun bullet) has described conditions in Greenwood; the widow of Louis Allen has recorded her trial by persecution; and SNCC worker McArthur Cotton has written about Parchman Penitentiary, where jailers hung him by his hands for three hours. The record is full of incidents such as these:

AFFIDAVIT OF JAMES BLACK.

On June 8, 1964, five COFO workers passed through Columbus carrying literature supporting Fannie Lou Hamer for Congress. Highway patrolmen stopped their car and said: "You goddam niggers want to change our way of life." This accusation, it seemed, was enough to cause the arrest of the workers. The sheriff of Lowndes County, called to the scene by the highway patrol, arrived and took four of the young men to jail. The highway patrolman led the fifth person, James Black, a seventeen-year-old-Negro boy, to a spot about a mile from where the car had been halted. According to Black's sworn testimony:

"He told me to get out of the car; I refused to get out. So he pulled me out. He started hitting me with his fists, and after about twenty blows he got out his blackjack and hit me one time with it and knocked me down. Then he told me to get back in the car. . . . Then he took me to the county jail where I was questioned by the sheriff. The sheriff asked for my driver's license and to take everything out of my pockets . . . I had a friend's I.D. card in my pocket and he asked me if my friend was a Negro or a nigger. I told him a Negro. The same highway patrolman was there, and took out his blackjack and again asked if my friend was a Negro or a nigger. He started to hit me with the blackjack, and I told him my friend was a nigger." [1] Black was tried the next day for "reckless driving," fined, and released.

AFFIDAVIT OF CHARLES MCLAURIN.

One of the men arrested with James Black was Charles McLaurin, twenty-three, a native Mississippi Negro who later served as a project director in Ruleville. McLaurin testified that the keepers of the Lowndes County jail systematically beat each man. The turnkey took the men one by one out of their cell for an "interview":

"I went out next and was taken outside. Elders [a highway patrolman] asked, 'Are you a Negro or a nigger?' I said, 'I am a Negro.' Jolly, another highway patrolman, hit me across the face with his forearm. Elders repeated the question and my answer was the same. I was then punched hard in my left ear by Elders and knocked to the ground. The highway patrolman helped me up and one of them said, 'Boy, can't you stand on your own two feet?' They stood me up against the wall and repeated the question.

"This time I answered, 'I am a nigger.' " [2]

AFFIDAVIT OF GREEN BREWER.

In another part of the state, Tallahatchie County, Negroes attempted to register to vote for the first time since Reconstruction days. A court order had enjoined county registrar William Cox to determine the qualifications of Negro registrants by the same standard as whites. Four men from the same Negro family, the Brewers of Charleston, were the first to try to register. In February of 1964, Green Brewer, twenty-nine, went to a neighborhood grocery store with his brother Charles. According to Green Brewer's affidavit:

"Charles went inside the store to get soft drinks. It seemed as if it was taking a long time for him to come out. . . . I then began to hear the sound of some licks. I ran inside the store and saw my brother Charles lying on the floor. He was bleeding. He was unconscious. Mr. Huntly [owner of the store] had backed up against the counter, holding an axe handle. Another white man, Mr. George Little, was also holding an axe handle.

". . . Mr. Huntly started to cuss me, saying I better get him out before I kill him . . . Mr. Huntly then got his gun—and started to shake—when I got a blow from behind. I received a fractured skull, broken jawbone, broken nose and a burst eyeball." [3]

About a week later, the sheriff, Alex Doghan, interviewed Green Brewer but, as Brewer put it, "since then nothing has happened on our behalf."

AFFIDAVIT OF WILLIAM ADAMS.

Another person in Tallahatchie, Ed Adams, also tried to register to vote. In his testimony, the young man's father, Mr. Williams Adams, described the punishment which his son received as a result of his action:

". . . I am a Negro citizen of the United States. I live on the Rabbit Ridge Plantation. . . . I and all my sons who are old enough work on this plantation. On August 11, 1964, my son, William Ed Adams, went to the County Courthouse to register to vote. He was seen by the crowd of whites who assembled in the courthouse square. Later that afternoon, Mr. Nelson Douglas, the manager of Rabbit Ridge Plantation, told some people at the plantation store that he was going to have my son arrested because he tried to register to vote.

". . . I went over to the store and saw Mr. Douglas. I asked, 'What are you going to have him arrested for? He hasn't done anything.'

"Mr. Douglas replied, 'He didn't have no business going down to the courthouse. He don't have no more work around here. We can't use a boy like that.' " [4]

William Adams tried to get his son reinstated but the owner of the Rabbit Ridge Plantation, J. Nolan Reed, said that unless the boy's name was removed from the voting rolls, he could not work on the plantation anymore.

AFFIDAVIT OF BEATRICE COLE.

On May 31, Michael Schwerner and James Chaney had spoken before a mass meeting at the Mt. Zion church in a rural section of Neshoba County. On June 16, whites burned the church to the ground and abducted the lay leader of the church, Junior Roosevelt Cole, a 58-year-old Negro. One gang of masked whites beat Mrs. Georgia Rush (a leader of the church) and her son while another group beat and kicked Mr. Cole. His wife, Beatrice Cole, said in her statement:

"There was at least 20 of them there. One of them pulled my husband out of the car and beat him, I couldn't see what with, but it looked like an iron object. Than they kicked him while he was lying on the ground. Then they said to him. 'Better say something or we'll kill you.' I said, 'He can't say nothing; he's unconscious.' Then I began to pray, a little prayer. They told me to shut my mouth. But I said, 'let me pray.' I stretched out my hands and said, 'Father, I stretch out my hand to thee; no other help I know; if thou withdrew thyself from me; Oh Lord, whither shall I go?'

"That struck the hearts of those men. The Lord was there, because then the man said. 'Let her alone' and he looked kind of sick about it.

"I think my husband's jaw is broken, because his teeth don't sit right in his mouth. But he doesn't think it is, and I can't get him to go down to the clinic again." [5]

These ordeals occur every day in Mississippi. This land of jack-booted terror is a place where the Negro who wishes to vote loses his job, where the police debase the Negro who refuses to describe himself as a "nigger," where hooded men torture church leaders. It is a regime of unrelenting brutality where many Negroes, like Beatrice Cole, feel that they have no shield except for their plaintive prayers. The rule of law can have no meaning in a state where a Federal judge, deciding a voter registration case, can refer from the bench to the applicants as "a bunch of niggers who are acting like a bunch of chimpanzees." [6]

Americans must soon come to realize, as one observer has put it, that "Mississippi 1964, is Germany, 1936, revisited." [7] And we cannot, like contemporary Germans, excuse ourselves with the alibi, "We didn't know."

What can be done to break the circle of fear, violence, and repression? Unfortunately, the situation is so bad that some commentators have abandoned hope. "Any scheme which holds out real hope for Mississippi's 900,000 black inhabitants is inherently improbable," *New Republic* editor Christopher Jencks felt forced to conclude after a visit to the state. "Probability is all on the side of despair." [8]

Negro leaders within the state—rightly, in my opinion—have not yet reached such a bleak conclusion. Citing the advances of 1964, they contend that Mississippi can be reformed by a judicious combination of persuasion, peaceful coercion, and force. Three possible strategies have been suggested:

1. The launching of armed guerrilla warfare aimed at undermining racist supremacy;

2. The strengthening and broadening of the nonviolent Negro

mass movement in the state, particularly by building an effective political force;

3. Decisive legal, political, and economic intervention by the federal government.

We must seriously consider each of these alternatives, for the fate of Mississippi's Negroes—and the vigor of American democracy—depends on which course is eventually followed.

Should Negroes Use Guns?

Let us examine the most radical possibility first: civil war as an instrument for ending white supremacy. At first glance, it might seem unlikely that Mississippi Negroes would turn to violence. They are outnumbered, their opponents control the police and National Guard, and white public opinion in the rest of the nation would unanimously condemn violence.

Negro strategists are aware of these facts and, in consequence, Mississippi Negroes demonstrated an almost superhuman restraint in the face of provocation. Only occasionally during the long, hot summer did they fire back at their attackers. Nonetheless, talk of violence was everywhere in the air.

At a meeting protesting the freeing of Byron de la Beckwith, one Jackson minister said: "We might have been in a segregated army, but we were all taught target practice. I hold an expert medal with the M-1 rifle, I hold a sharpshooter medal with the '03 Springfield, and I hold a marksman medal with the carbine." Particularly among veterans, the desire ran strong to retaliate against the police and the Klansmen. Yet they restrained themselves.

For several reasons, I doubt that the Negro self-control of the early 1960's will continue indefinitely. If you are tortured, the normal reaction is to retaliate. Why should we expect Negroes to inhibit this natural human tendency? Further, it must be realized that many Negroes believe that they could win a violent confrontation with whites. As several studies have shown, a significant proportion of Negroes believe that they are tougher, stronger, and better able to stand pain than are whites.[9] And, incredibly, some Negroes think that whites in America are in a minority. Thus, the practical arguments condemning violence as inexpedient carry little weight in this segment of the population.

It should be emphasized, too, that these opinions about Negro strength are most commonly found in the less educated section of the population. It is exactly this group which has increasingly joined in the Mississippi revolt. Despite the rational arguments of Negro leaders, the rank and file of the movement may well take to violence as a last desperate resort against tyranny.

Even Bob Moses—an eminently realistic leader, dedicated in almost saintly fashion to a peaceful approach—has publicly implied that the Negroes' patience might finally be exhausted. In an interview during the summer, Moses was asked what would happen if legal action failed to stop the subterfuge and intimidation which prevent Mississippi Negroes from voting. He replied, "We'd set up our own election, call in observers, and ask that we be recognized as the true government of Mississippi." [10] To enforce such a declaration of independence would, of course, require armed strength.

Would the use of violence inevitably fail? We must face this question in all seriousness. Many American liberals find it distasteful even to consider violence as a way of guaranteeing Negro rights. Yet these same people often look to the American Revolution, the European resistance to Nazism, or the freedom fighters in Hungary as glorious examples of the will to freedom. The moral right of Negroes to revolt against white terrorism and a corrupt legal system is, for me, beyond debate: a resort to arms in defense of liberty would be morally justifiable if peaceful attempts to bring change have failed. The only real issue is whether violence would worsen or improve the Negroes' condition.

Those who advocate armed self-defense (and their numbers are increasing) put forward several arguments. They begin with the pessimistic assumption that the federal government will not take the steps necessary to topple the racists from power as long as an atmosphere of outward tranquility prevails in Mississippi. They point to the impossibility of bringing racists to judgment for their atrocities; the laggard pace of the Justice Department in protecting civil rights workers, and the difficulty in getting large numbers of Negro voters enrolled at the polls. The nonviolent approach, some Negro leaders contend, fails when it attempts to change the structure of southern political power or the basic economic pattern of the region; it works only when attacking the periphery of segregation. Thus, they say, a few restaurants may be opened to middle-class Negroes by a nonviolent approach, but the method cannot secure the conviction of a brutal sheriff, or alter the plantation system, or give the vote to more than a token number of Negroes.

The alternative would be to strike back in a planned, selective fashion against the white tyranny. Such a battle, some Negro leaders have suggested in private, would take three forms:

1. ARMED DEFENSE OF HOMES. In response to direct attacks on their persons or property, Negroes would organize self-defense leagues. When flagrant abuses occurred—a cross-burning in Carthage, a bombing in McComb, a church-burning in Natchez—Negroes would fire back at their attackers. Such a program would require the establishment of armed night patrols (which already exist in some towns) to mount a defense ring around Negro neighborhoods and particularly vulnerable targets. This policy, its proponents say, could deter whites from violent forays.

2. VIGILANTE ACTION. Literally hundreds of whites have beaten or killed Negroes and have never been brought to trial for their crimes. Even if they have made a token appearance before the courts, the white juries and judges have almost always acquitted

them.* Negroes know who killed Medgar Evers and Mack Parker; who beat James Black, Charles McLaurin, Green Brewer, and Roosevelt Cole; they know who murdered James Chaney, Michael Schwerner, and Andrew Goodman. The angry men in Negro ranks wish to bring these whites to justice, to pay them back an eye for an eye for their crimes. They propose that vigilante courts be set up which would try these men and administer justice.

3. ECONOMIC SABOTAGE. Some of the advocates of armed rebellion propose a selective campaign of terrorism against those plantations, businesses, and factories whose owners have most blatantly maltreated Negroes. In its extreme form, this would mean that a plantation owner who fires a Negro for voting would find his cotton gin blown up the next day or that an auxiliary policeman who attacks a Negro woman would have his store burned to the ground.

Its advocates maintain that this guerrilla warfare would not be conducted in the random fashion of Harlem riots. Rather, it would be tied to a series of specific demands made on the white population. If the whites acceded to the Negro requests—if they would assure protection of life and property, access to the vote, and equality of opportunity—the war would, in theory, end.

The policy of guerrilla warfare has certain important advantages. It is a program which could be carried out by a small, determined group of men. It would strike back directly at those oppressors who have so far waged a one-sided war with a blithe disregard for consequences. It would inevitably focus national and world attention on Mississippi in unprecedented fashion.

But here is the difficulty: the black men of Mississippi just cannot mobilize enough armed power to overthrow their white

---

* Indeed, after his trial, Byron de la Beckwith, accused murderer of Medgar Evers, received $25,000 from the U.S. Post Office Department for some property he owns.

masters. Certainly, Negroes have the capacity and right to defend their homes against bombings. It is imperative that every Negro family in Mississippi be armed, that every Negro block have its warning system, that every Negro church be provided with armed watchmen. Only universal armed vigilance in the community will successfully defend the people against sneak attacks. Nevertheless, a full-scale policy of armed rebellion, one which incorporated so-called acts of aggression as well as defense, could not fulfill its goals.

Inevitably, the violence would escalate, and whites would retaliate massively with all the weapons at their disposal. Northern liberals, shocked at the use of violence, would cry for a restoration of "law and order," while the nation's reactionaries would demand iron-fisted repression. Federal troops might well be called in, but their purpose would be to repress the Negro revolt, not to enforce civil rights. Mississippi is not France under the Nazis or even South Africa under the Afrikaners. The Negroes could never expect foreign assistance to their rebellion. They would be decimated and go down in a defeat as abysmal as that suffered by the Warsaw underground in World War II. If "the fire next time" starts, it would be a futile gesture against injustice, which, in the end, would bring catastrophe to the Negro cause.

The only way to avoid disaster is to give Mississippi Negroes a major voice in their destinies before they give up hope in the possibilities of peaceful progress and turn to violence. Most of Mississippi's current Negro leadership believes that there still may be time to create a formidable but nonviolent reform movement in the state before an armed rebellion begins.

"Limited Coercion": The Possibilities of Nonviolent Action

For 1964, the Negro leaders of Mississippi eschewed the path of armed violence and hoped instead to intensify their political, legal, and educational campaigns against the white overlords. The policy of men like Aaron Henry, Charles Evers, and Robert Moses has been labeled as one of "limited coercion": a program of agitation, boycotts, protests, demonstrations, and legal action designed to make life so unpleasant for the whites that they will eventually turn to compromise rather than massive resistance. The Negro leaders, for the most part, do not cling to a Gandhian hope of somehow "changing the hearts" of white segregationists; rather, they hope to force them—in a peaceful manner, to be sure—to the point of negotiation.

The policy which guides COFO has two goals: a realignment of political power in the state and a tangible improvement in the economic lot of Negroes.* To implement its policy, COFO will have at its disposal ninety-five regular staff members. In addition, two hundred northern volunteers who had come to Mississippi for the summer of 1964 were so horrified by conditions there that they decided to remain for at least another year's "hitch." Several thousand other people have indicated their willingness to come to Mississippi on a volunteer basis for a minimum of three months. Several religious, medical, and legal organizations have made a permanent commitment to altering the Mississippi way of life. COFO's mass support will come from tens of thousands of Negroes—and perhaps, hundreds of thousands of them in the not too distant future.

During the rest of the 1960's, the Negro movement in Mississippi plans to undertake these specific tasks:

* By its nature, COFO is such an amorphous organization that one can hardly talk of its policy. The tactics, let alone the strategy, of COFO leaders, change constantly—partially in response to the demands of the situation, partially because of the conflicting pressure groups operating within the organization. When I speak of policy, therefore, I mean only the broad lines of action which COFO has followed in the past and proposes publicly to follow in the future. Further, it should be noted that unfortunate conflicts divide COFO from some other Negro groups in the state. The NAACP, for example, is technically a member of COFO but often follows its own separate program. These fratricidal conflicts must be healed if the Negro movement is going to sweep to success.

—Intensification of voter campaigns: certain counties, recently opened up by court orders, will be the object of voter registration campaigns. Panola and Tallahatchie Counties will be special targets. In such sections of Mississippi, Negroes have not tried to register since the Civil War; it requires unique courage to take the risk. (In Tallahatchie, twenty-four Negroes registered during the summer of 1964, although armed whites gathered to intimidate them.)

—Freedom schools will continue in twenty-one communities. Community centers will operate in twenty towns.

—Preschool day-care centers will be established in several areas of the state.

—Libraries will be built in every community center, and mobile libraries will tour distant rural areas.

—Special instructors will work with rural Negroes, explaining the benefits of various federal programs (antipoverty measures, public health programs, housing and consumer projects). Whites have been able to withhold the benefits of these federal programs partially because of Negro ignorance; the hope in the future is to inform every farming Negro of his rights to participate.

—Lawyers provided by the Lawyer's Constitutional Defense Committee and the Lawyer's Guild will be permanently stationed in the state to defend Negro civil rights.* White prosecutors, accustomed to dealing with undefended victims, will find themselves challenged on major and minor legal points.

—Food and clothing will be distributed to people who have suffered economic harassment for activity in the Negro revolt or who are economically destitute for other reasons.

—New medical programs, sponsored by the Medical Committee

* The Lawyer's Guild has been labelled as "Communist" by various congressional committees. Indeed, some northern liberal lawyers balked at the idea of COFO accepting aid from a group which has so often been tainted with the Communist accusation. Yet, in the Mississippi situation, COFO had to welcome help from any legal source and the Lawyer's Guild has done yeoman service in aiding defenseless Negroes.

on Human Rights, will be initiated. Northern doctors will work with Mississippi Negroes on problems of public health, diet, prenatal care, and first aid.

This is the program for the remaining part of the decade. It is ambitiously conceived and, with the relatively meager resources available for the program, can go far in helping Mississippi Negroes. Though important in themselves, these projects are merely part of a much grander plan: an attempt to restructure the entire social and political system of Mississippi.* As Bob Moses has remarked, "This movement is pointed . . . not toward the downtown whites but toward the rural Negro, not toward acceptance by the white community but toward the organization of political and other kinds of expression in the Negro community, or really toward the organization of a Negro society." [11]

The political realignment envisioned by Negro leaders will, in theory, be spearheaded by the Freedom Democratic party. COFO men envisage a massive registration of Negro voters (either on "freedom ballots" or real registration tallies) who—when allied with labor union groups, poor whites, and some white moderates —would succeed in forming a major pressure group within the state. For the immediate future, the hope is that the Freedom party will have enough political leverage to influence the policies of the regular Democratic machine. Eventually, perhaps, the Freedom Democrats might replace the regular party and thereby gain the privileges of federal patronage. The Freedom party would use its control of federal offices and federal spending to initiate fundamental social changes within Mississippi.

This vision of the future—which I have stated in the most con-

---

* Some COFO leaders, particularly SNCC workers, have even more radical plans. They wish to remake all of America along more equalitarian and socialist lines. They would welcome a radical revival in America, a more just redistribution of wealth, a new atmosphere of brotherhood, and a foreign policy based on friendship with nationalist and revolutionary movements throughout the world. They are hostile to the middle class, hostile toward the white man, hostile toward capitalism. They have no desire for integration into a world characterized by Harlems and South Side Chicagos.

servative terms used by COFO leaders—is based on two premises: first, that a large segment of Negroes can in fact secure the right to vote and, secondly, that the Freedom party can attract a significant number of poor whites to its ranks. These assumptions require careful scrutiny.

In order to make Negroes a powerful part of the electorate, Mississippi will have to repeal most of its electoral laws and radically change its practice of persecuting potential Negro voters. The law requiring an "interpretation" of the Mississippi constitution would have to go; discriminating registrars would have to be vigorously prosecuted; the FBI or federal marshals would have to investigate all charges of intimidation; and various subtle ways of preventing Negro registration (such as an ordinance requiring that the names of all would-be voters must be published) would have to be invalidated.

Let us assume, however, that a revolution in electoral practices did occur. Under present national law, this radical change would still allow only 50 per cent of the eligible Negro population to vote. The Civil Rights Law requires a sixth-grade education or its equivalent as a qualification for voting. Because of inferior schooling, because many have been forced to work in the fields early in life, and because the better-educated Negroes have flocked to the North's relative freedom, only half of the adult Negroes in Mississippi could qualify under the current rules. Thus, even if Mississippi followed a completely fair procedure in registering voters, Negroes would constitute only 21 per cent of the voting public.

I do not wish to minimize the importance of voting: in those counties where Negroes are in a majority (and usually these are the areas where whites are most cruelly on the rampage), the Negro voting bloc could still have great significance in affecting the election of local officers. The county sheriffs and judges, all of whom are elected, would have to modify their more brutal practices if they wished to be returned to public office. On a statewide level, the fact that Negroes make up only one-fifth of the presently eligible voting population means that Negroes must make an alliance with some section of the white people. "A liberal Democratic coalition would have to win the allegiance of about 40 per cent of the state's white voters in order to capture statewide office," Christopher Jencks has correctly observed. "At present it is hard to imagine a candidate who could both win support from Negro voters and from 40 per cent of the whites." [12]

Since Negroes are, inescapably, a minority, their leaders have undertaken a remarkable campaign to join together poor whites and poor Negroes in a single political unit. Workers have moved out into twenty counties, trying to convert lower-class whites to the Freedom party. Reminiscent of the Populist era, COFO literature tells white farmers, "We must be allies . . . race has led us both to poverty."

The attempt to proselytize poor whites is based on some rather naïve Marxist preconceptions. About 70,000 white families in Mississippi earn less than $2,000 a year. Because "the poor have the political need of decent jobs, housing, education, and health," some COFO leaders believe that they will gladly join with the Negro mass movement to end the curse of poverty.[13] In making this assumption, COFO leaders completely ignore the lessons of history.

Man's paramount political need is for dignity. Next to religion, a feeling of race superiority satisfies this longing. Exactly because the poor whites are economically deprived (and because even they can no longer take religion very seriously), they are the group most likely to express politically their virulent Negro hatred. The "objective" similarity of poor whites to poor Negroes has nothing to do with their motivation: it is exactly this similarity which drives the poor white, subjectively, to emphasize his racial superiority. This attempt to win over the white proletariat is, I fear, doomed to failure.

COFO's emphasis on converting the poor whites (as well as the usual tradition of American radicalism that the middle class cannot act as an agent of change) has resulted in creating a gulf between white Mississippi moderates and the Negro mass movement.

"The important work to be done is with poor folks and not with moderates and liberals," COFO literature announces—and yet the exact opposite is true. Politically, the only possible white allies of the Negro movement will be the middle-class, educated moderates such as "The Mississippians for Public Education." The prime political task is to forge a workable alliance with these moderates who, as a result of the events of 1964, have just begun to exercise their latent power.

However one assesses the combination of forces at work within Mississippi, the chances that the Negro revolt can, by its own effort, achieve victory seem dim indeed. COFO can educate Negroes, alleviate their poverty slightly, provide some legal protections, and improve their health. The Freedom party will, in time, create a pressure group of Negro voters which can sway, but hardly control, the state's politics. The white moderates, if they can conquer their fears, might see to it that school integration proceeds and that Negroes win an increasingly important part in state politics.

All of this is needed. All of it is important. Yet it is not enough. What must be done—and what can be done if Americans have the vision—is to remove Mississippi from the arena of sectional problems and place it where it belongs: in the forefront of the issues confronting all Americans.

A Task for the Nation

Whites will not change Mississippi voluntarily; and Negroes do not have the power to reform the state. Only the entire American people, acting through the federal government, can bring about the downfall of the Mississippi tyranny.

National leaders have hesitated to take those steps which would ensure that Mississippi Negroes could practice their rights to life, liberty, and the pursuit of happiness. Admittedly, the federal government has helped by identifying some of the racial murderers, by providing a legal basis for school desegregation, and by paving the way for free access to public accommodations. But these measures, while laudable, do little for the overwhelming majority of Negroes. A Negro in Mississippi cannot speak freely. He cannot vote freely. He cannot assemble freely. He cannot rest securely in the peace of his home.

America's leaders in the 1960's may have been aware of these facts, but they still failed to act decisively. In August, 1964, Attorney General Robert Kennedy expressed the opinion that the situation in Mississippi was "a local matter for law enforcement." * And the director of the FBI (while visiting in Mississippi) announced that it was not his job to protect civil rights workers. He insisted that "the Bureau is for investigation, not enforcement."

The hesitancy of national leaders to intervene in Mississippi has, supposedly, been due to a lack of legal justification for violating a state's integrity. This is a specious argument. Under section 333 of Title 10 of the Federal Code, the President is empowered "to take such action as he considers necessary to suppress, in any state, any insurrection, domestic violence, unlawful combination, or conspiracy, if it . . . opposes or obstructs the execution of the laws of the United States." Since 1879, the Supreme Court has con-

---

* Almost immediately after the Attorney General's statement, the quality of "local law enforcement" was amply demonstrated in McComb. During a single day in September, the home of a Negro ex-police officer was bombed (he had testified before the Civil Rights Advisory Committee); the home of another Negro was bombed; and police arrested twenty-four Negroes under the state's "criminal syndicalism" law, an omnibus law designed to punish "subversives." Dennis Sweeny, a COFO staff member who had been a victim of an earlier bombing, was arrested as an "accessory after the fact" and for possession of dynamite. He was released on $5,000 bail when the police, by their own admission, failed to frighten any of the local Negroes into testifying against him.

sistently upheld the federal government's right to take "police action" in any state where lawlessness prevails.

"We hold it to be an incontrovertible principle," Mr. Justice Bradley stated in 1879, "that the government of the United States may, by means of physical force, exercised through its official agents, execute on every foot of American soil the functions that belong to it." (*Ex parte Siebold,* 100 U.S. 371, 394–95.) The law is straightforward: the government of the United States has the legal right to take whatever action necessary to guarantee that the nation's laws will be faithfully executed in every state of the union.

Only a strong show of federal power will make the nation's laws operative in Mississippi. In the spirit of President Johnson's plea to "close the springs of racial poison . . . and make our nation whole," the federal government must act to free Mississippi from its diseased racism.* There are three ways in which the federal government can effectively intervene: the government can ensure essential civil liberties for Negroes; the government can guarantee the right to vote, and the government can strike at the root injustices underlying the Negro revolt by improving the economic condition of the black inhabitants.

FEDERAL PROTECTION OF BASIC RIGHTS. The federal government has allowed Mississippi to flaunt national law. The government has not even tried to protect the lives, liberty, or property of those engaged in the civil rights revolt—a revolt aimed at fulfilling rather than subverting the United States Constitution. The FBI has acted reluctantly and only under great pressure. (The agency entered the case of the murdered civil rights workers only after twenty hours and sixteen telephone calls had been expended

* On several occasions in the past, similar pleas have been made. On January 29, 1884, Senator John Sherman introduced a resolution in the U.S. Senate calling for federal action to preserve the law in Mississippi. He argued that "when the essential rights of citizenship are overthrown in a state," the national government had the duty to intervene. The Senate ignored the plight of Mississippi's Negroes then and on subsequent occasions.

in trying to gain its cooperation.)

The government's excuse has been that convictions could not be obtained, even if national agencies made arrests. This is true but does not excuse inaction. The government can prosecute people under the civil rights law without requiring the services of local district attorneys; it can initiate mass arrests which, whatever their outcome, could serve to deter some white extremists; it could so infiltrate the towns of Mississippi that violent action by segregationists would become almost impossible; and, if all else failed, martial law could be imposed on those areas, like the town of McComb, where preventive legal action has clearly been inadequate.

I am advocating here only the most elementary precautions. The killings must stop. The bombings must stop. The burnings and beatings must stop. Local authorities are either unwilling or unable to end the racist rampage. Indeed, a major task in itself is to place federal forces in a position where they can oversee, control, and punish local police who violate the law. There is only one workable alternative: the federal government must dispatch U.S. Marshals, and if necessary, U.S. troops to end Mississippi's flagrant and systematic violation of basic human rights.

FEDERAL PROTECTION OF THE RIGHT TO VOTE. Almost one hundred years ago, Americans added the Fifteenth Amendment to our Constitution. Its language is admirably brief and pointed: "The right of citizens of the United States to vote shall not be denied or abridged by the United States or by any State on account of race, color or previous condition of servitude."

The ruling whites in Mississippi have consistently disobeyed this law. Various approaches have been tried to stop their actions, but these measures have not yet had a discernible effect. Only federal action can buttress the law. These are the steps which ought to be followed:

—Invoke existing legislation to enjoin all county registrars from discriminating against Negroes.

—Enforce the law by placing federal referees at every registration place and every voting booth.

—Protect Negro voters with armed federal marshals or federal troops.

—Ensure that white Mississippi politicians stand for "law and order" by informing them that federal patronage depends upon their cooperation with the national government.

—Launch a literacy program for adult Negroes to make up for deficiencies in their education.

The choice is clear: either America takes actions such as these to make Negroes full, voting citizens, or Mississippi will maintain its white dictatorship with all the force at its disposal.

FEDERAL ACTION TO END NEGRO POVERTY. We should go beyond assuring constitutional rights and an open field for electoral battle. These advances are of undeniable importance, but—in attempting to repay Negroes for generations of slavery, indignity, and brutality—America must act boldly to assure genuine equality of opportunity.*

There should be no further reason for passivity. The means for progress exist if America has sufficient will to use them. We, as Americans, can undertake many tangible steps:

We can see to it that Negro babies in Mississippi will have a life expectancy which approaches that of whites by initiating an extensive program of public health.

We can build truly representative local groups to establish small rural industries and area improvement projects everywhere in the

---

* A realist has to admit the tragic fact that America can never fully repay the debt it owes to Mississippi Negroes. Even the most heroic measures are unlikely to change totally the legacy of Negro servitude: Negro families, in the foreseeable future, will continue to earn much less than whites. Negroes will still be dependent on the whims of white employers. Negroes will still have to subsist on the pleasure of white storekeepers. Short of a total revolution, one cannot expect these fundamental social and economic relationships to change.

state.

We can intensify those programs which will give the Mississippi Negroes a fairer economic opportunity by broadening the area redevelopment plans, by offering manpower retraining, and by furthering a creative public works program.

We can extend and fortify the gains made in school integration, by pressing every Mississippi county to end all school segregation now.

We can, while opening the public purse for legitimate programs, forbid the use of federal funds for the perpetuation of segregation in Mississippi: no federal money for segregated schools, housing, agricultural projects, or community facilities.

We can see to it that the withholding of federal aid (as in rural relief programs) will not be used as an instrument to intimidate Negroes who attempt to vote or to assert their rights in other ways.

The federal government can, in effect, exert pressure all along the economic front to end racism in Mississippi and to build a southern society where poverty has finally been eradicated.

This list of America's responsibilities could go on much further, for the federal government, if it so wished, could end Mississippi's most obvious abuses tomorrow. The government could see to it that the law is enforced, it could use federal aid to help Negroes, and it could cease to bolster the whites' dictatorship. All of these things must be done with whatever means the situation requires and circumstances allow.

In this time of national choice, we would do well to remember the pleas made long ago by Mississippi's Negro statesman, Senator B. K. Bruce. During the 1870's, Bruce repeatedly protested Mississippi's degradation of its Negro citizens. In condemning conditions similar to those that prevail in Mississippi today, Bruce argued that "the sober American judgement must obtain in the South as elsewhere in the Republic." He warned the American people that Mississippi Negroes would not forever wait in passive obedience to see their dreams fulfilled: "It will not accord with the laws of nature or history to brand colored people a race of cowards. On more than one historic field, they have attested in blood their courage as well as a love of liberty. I ask Senators to believe that no consideration of fear or personal danger has kept us quiet and forbearing under the provocations and wrongs that have so sorely tried our souls." [14]

In response to their degraded station in life, Negroes avoided responding with violence, Bruce said, only because "we determined to wait until such time as an appeal to the good sense and justice of the American people could be made." [15] Fundamentally, Senator Bruce had faith in the promises of America and the future of his people. "I have confidence," he affirmed, "not only in my country and her institutions, but in the endurance, capacity and destiny of my people. . . . Whatever our ultimate position in the composite civilization of the Republic and whatever varying fortunes attend our career, we will not forget our instincts for freedom nor our love for country." [16]

The time has come for white Americans to justify the faith which Senator Bruce and other Negro Americans have placed in our Constitution, our Declaration of Independence, and our Emancipation Proclamation.

In Mississippi, in America as a whole, we face a moral challenge where the alternatives are clear: either the supremacy of national law is upheld or we descend rapidly into anarchic violence. All of us—from the President down to a freedom school teacher —have a moral commitment to ensure that the hundreds who have died in Mississippi did not perish in vain. To be sure, the time ahead will be full of frustration and discord and danger. But, as President John Kennedy said in pleading for the cause of civil rights, "Those who do nothing are inviting shame as well as violence. Those who act boldly are recognizing right as well as reality."

All Americans have an engagement in Mississippi. In the spirit of the late President, let us meet it nobly and courageously.

Notes

CHAPTER 1

1. COFO press release, April, 1964 (mimeo.).
2. "Prospectus for the Summer," COFO, Jackson, Miss., April, 1964 (mimeo.).
3. Quoted in "Freedom Booklet," COFO, Jackson, Miss., July, 1964.
4. Quoted in *Mississippi: The Closed Society* by James W. Silver (New York: Harcourt, Brace & World, Inc., 1964), pp. 101 and 102.
5. *Ibid.*, p. 90.
6. Quoted in David Halberstam, "The Mississippi Primaries: Delay and 'Cousin Plemon. . . ." *The Reporter*, Sept. 22, 1955, p. 31.
7. See "A Chronology of Violence and Intimidation in Mississippi Since 1961" by Jack Mirmis (mimeo.), COFO, for a complete record. Submitted in the *Congressional Record*, April 4, 1963.
8. Quoted in Silver, *op. cit.*, p. 91.
9. "A Chronology of Violence and Intimidation in Mississippi Since 1961," *op. cit.*
10. Jeannine Herron, "Underground Election," *The Nation*, May 18, 1964, p. 502.
11. *Ibid.*, p. 389.
12. Quoted in "Incident in Hattiesburg" by Howard Zinn, *The Nation*, May 18, 1964, p. 502.
13. Norman Thomas, quoted in "Underground Election," *op. cit.*, p. 389.
14. *Case Studies of Intimidation*, COFO, Jackson, Miss., July, 1964 (mimeo.).

211

15. Quoted in Silver, *op. cit.,* pp. 101–102.
16. Cited in the *Memphis Commercial Appeal,* Jan. 15, 1962.
17. "The General Condition of the Mississippi Negro," COFO, Jackson, Miss., 1964 (mimeo.).
18. Quoted in Silver, *op. cit.,* p. 19.
19. *Ibid.,* p. 25.
20. Medford Evans, "The Five-Point Action Program," *The Citizen,* The Citizens' Council, Jackson, Miss., Jan., 1964, pp. 11–15.
21. Quoted in "A County Divided Against Itself," by David Halberstam, *The Reporter,* Dec. 15, 1955, p. 31.
22. *Ibid.,* p. 32.
23. *Ibid.,* p. 32.
24. For evidence see "COFO's Proposed Community Centers" Jackson, Miss., 1964 (mimeo.), and "The General Condition of the Mississippi Negro," COFO, Jackson, Miss., 1964 (mimeo.).
25. "Tired of Being Sick and Tired," by Jeny De Muth, *The Nation,* June 1, 1964.
26. *Ibid.*
27. *Ibid.*
28. *Ibid.*
29. *Ibid.*
30. "Overview of the Freedom Schools," COFO, Jackson, Miss., 1964 (mimeo.).
31. Quoted in "It Will Be a Hot Summer in Mississippi," by Richard Woodley, *The Reporter,* May 21, 1964.
32. Charles J. Benner in a letter to James Forman, June 16, 1964.
33. "Tired of Being Sick and Tired," *op. cit.*

CHAPTER 2

1. Quoted in "If We Can Crack Mississippi . . ." by James Atwater, *The Saturday Evening Post,* July 25, 1964, p. 16.
2. *Ibid.,* p. 17.
3. Quoted in *Newsweek,* July 13, 1964, p. 20.
4. Quoted in "It Will Be a Hot Summer in Mississippi," by Richard Woodley, *The Reporter,* May 21, 1964.
5. Quoted in "If We Can Crack Mississippi . . . ," *op. cit.*
6. George Keith, "Bite Your Lip," *The Carthaginian,* Carthage, Miss., July 2, 1964.
7. Jimmy Ward, "Covering the Cross Roads," *Jackson Daily News,* July 16, 1964.
8. Quoted in "Mississippi's Press vs. Invaders" by Claude Sitton, *San Francisco Chronicle,* June 30, 1964, p. 9.
9. Quoted in "Students Open Dixie Crusade," *Palo Alto Times,* June 23, 1964, p. 4.
10. *Ibid.*
11. "Wrong Targets Criticized" by Joseph Alsop, syndicated column, June 24, 1964.
12. Field Report to COFO, June 29, 1964, Jackson, Miss.
13. Described in "If We Can Crack Mississippi . . . ," *op. cit.*

14. Field report to COFO, June 23, 1964, Jackson, Miss.
15. Quoted in *Newsweek*, *op. cit.*, p. 18.
16. "Summary of Incidents," COFO, Jackson Miss., 1964 (mimeo.).
17. *Ibid.*
18. "How Negro Democrats Fared," COFO, Jackson, Miss., 1964, affidavit of Mr. Robert Lanier (mimeo.).
19. Frank Trippet, "An Account of Some Conversations on U.S. 45," *Newsweek*, July 13, 1964, p. 21.
20. *Ibid.*
21. *Ibid.*
22. "Missing Mississippi Summer Project Workers," COFO, Jackson, Miss., 1964 (mimeo.).

CHAPTER 3

1. Quoted in *Newsweek*, July 13, 1964, p. 20.
2. Quoted in "If We Can Crack Mississippi . . . ," by James Atwater, *Saturday Evening Post*, July 25, 1964.
3. *The Freedom Fighter*, Klu Klux Klan, Dec., 1963.
4. "The Most Awful Disease of Our Time," pamphlet, The White Knights of the Ku Klux Klan of Mississippi, summer, 1964.
5. Unidentified origin.
6. Atwater, *op. cit.*
7. Kenneth Tolliver, "New Racist Organization Terrorizes Several South Mississippi Counties," *The Delta Democrat-Times*, Greenville, Miss. (reproduced).
8. *Ibid.*
9. Quoted in Atwater, *op. cit.*
10. Resolution of the Mississippi House of Representatives, July 8, 1964.

CHAPTER 4

1. Governor Paul Johnson, United Press International release, Aug. 10, 1964.
2. Congressman Arthur Winstead, *Jackson Daily News*, Aug. 6, 1964.
3. Quoted in *Newsweek*, Aug. 17, 1964.
4. *Ibid.*
5. *Ibid.*
6. United Press International release, Aug. 6, 1964.
7. *Newsweek*, *op. cit.*
8. Quoted in *Neither Black Nor White*, by Wilma Dykeman and James Stokely (New York: Holt, Rinehart & Winston, Inc., 1957), p. 56.
9. Quoted in *The Southern Temper*, by William Peters (Garden City, N.Y.: Doubleday & Co., 1959), p. 45.
10. *Ibid.*
11. See J. C. Furnass, "Goodbye to Uncle Tom" (New York: William Sloane, 1956).
12. See William McCord and N. J. Demarath, "Negro versus White Intelligence," *Harvard Educational Review*, spring, 1958.
13. United Press International release, Aug. 24, 1964.
14. James Quigley, *Jackson Clarion-Ledger*, July 8, 1964.

15. Quoted in *Newsweek*, Sept. 10, 1964, p. 23–24.
16. Peter Weiss, "Nightmare in Mississippi," *The Progressive*, Sept., 1964, p. 20.
17. Robert Moses, quoted in *Newsweek*, Aug. 24, 1964, p. 18.
18. *Ibid.*, p. 20.
19. Southern Regional Council survey.
20. Moses, *op. cit.*, p. 18.
21. *Newsweek*, Aug. 31, 1964, p. 56.
22. *Ibid.*
23. Grenville Clark, letter to *The New York Times*, Aug. 16, 1964.
24. Reported in *Running Summary of Incidents*, COFO, Jackson, Miss., Sept., 1964.

CHAPTER 5

1. James Silver, *Mississippi: The Closed Society* (New York: Harcourt, Brace & World, Inc., 1964), p. 156.
2. William Brink and Louis Harris, *The Negro Revolution in America* (New York: Simon and Schuster, 1964), Chapter 9.
3. Letter to the Editor, *Jackson Daily News*, July 16, 1964.
4. Letter to the Editor, *Jackson Daily News*, July 20, 1964.
5. Letter to the Editor, *Jackson Daily News*, July 11, 1964.
6. "The Most Awful Disease of Our Time," Ku Klux Klan, Mississippi.
7. W. J. Simmons, "Organization: The Key to Victory," *The Citizen*, 1962, Jackson, Miss.
8. Manning Johnson, *Color, Communism and Common Sense*, American Opinion reprint series, Robert Welch, Inc., Belmont, Mass., 1958.
9. Cited in Silver, *op. cit.*, p. 54.
10. *Ibid.*, p. 67.
11. James Eastland, quoted in *Neither Black Nor White*, by Wilma Dykeman and James Stokely (New York: Holt, Rinehart & Winston, Inc., 1957), pp. 231–32.
12. Silver, *op. cit.*, pp. 42–43.
13. Quoted in Silver, *ibid.*, p. 42.
14. Mrs. A. J. Noel, letter to the editor, *Jackson Daily News*, July 10, 1964.
15. Mrs. Bruce Cooper, letter to the editor, *Jackson Daily News*, July 6, 1964.
16. Brink and Harris, *op. cit.*, Chapter 9.
17. Ralph McGill, syndicated column, June 27, 1964.
18. William Lee Miller, "People in Mississippi," *The Reporter*, Dec. 15, 1955, p. 28.
19. P. D. East, quoted in *Black Like Me* by John Howard Griffin (New York: Signet Books, 1961), p. 74.
20. Reproduced in "The Iconoclast of Petal, Mississippi," by Albert Vorspan, *The Reporter*, Mar. 21, 1957, p. 35.
21. *Ibid.*, p. 34.
22. *Ibid.*, p. 34.
23. Quoted in *Black Like Me*, *op. cit.*, p. 75.
24. Quoted in "The Iconoclast of Petal, Mississippi," *op. cit.*

25. Griffin, *op. cit.*, p. 76.
26. Hazel B. Smith, quoted in *The Southern Temper* by William Peters (Garden City, N.Y.: Doubleday & Company, Inc.: 1959), p. 31.
27. *Ibid.*
28. Silver, *op. cit.*, p. 155.
29. *Ibid.*, p. x.
30. Silver, *op. cit.*, p. xvi.
31. William Faulkner, quoted in Silver, *ibid.*, p. xii.
32. Louis Lomax, *The Negro Revolt* (New York: Signet Books, 1962), p. 257.

CHAPTER 6

1. Wilma Dykeman and James Stokely, *Neither Black Nor White* (New York: Holt, Rinehart & Winston, Inc., 1957), p. 60.
2. "Can We Meet this Challenge?" National Sharecroppers' Fund pamphlet, New York, 1964.
3. H. H. Humes quoted in *Mississippi: The Closed Society* by James Silver (New York: Harcourt, Brace & World, Inc., 1964), p. 88.
4. Medgar Evers, "Why I Live in Mississippi," *Ebony*, September, 1963, p. 144.
5. *Ibid.*, p. 144.
6. *Ibid.*, p. 45.
7. *Ibid.*, p. 147.
8. *Ibid.*, p. 148.
9. *Ibid.*, p. 148.

CHAPTER 7

1. Affidavit of James Black, sworn and witnessed, June 8, 1964.
2. Affidavit of Charles McLaurin, sworn and witnessed, June 8, 1964.
3. Affidavit of Green Brewer, sworn and witnessed, Aug., 1964.
4. Affidavit of Williams Adams, sworn and witnessed, Aug. 13, 1964.
5. Affidavit of Beatrice Cole, sworn and witnessed, June, 1964.
6. Quoted in "Nightmare in Mississippi" by Peter Weiss, *The Progressive*, September, 1964, p. 22.
7. *Ibid.*
8. Christopher Jencks, "Mississippi: From Conversion to Coercion," *The New Republic*, Aug. 22, 1964, p. 20.
9. See *The Negro Revolution in Amercia* by William Brink and Louis Harris (New York: Simon and Schuster, 1964).
10. Robert Moses, quoted in "Letter from Jackson" by Calvin Trillin, *The New Yorker*, Aug. 29, 1964, p. 103.
11. *Ibid.*, p. 92.
12. Jencks, *op cit.*, p. 21.
13. "We Must Be Allies," COFO, Jackson, Miss., Sept., 1964.
14. Senator Blanche K. Bruce, speech before the Senate on resolution to investigate election practices in Mississippi, Mar. 31, 1876.
15. *Ibid.*
16. *Ibid.*

INDEX